B & T
$3.50

D1269608

RELIGIOUS LANGUAGE

General editors of this book and others in the *Issues in Relgious Studies* series: Peter Baelz and Jean Holm

RELIGIOUS LANGUAGE

Peter Donovan

HAWTHORN BOOKS, INC.
Publishers/NEW YORK

Wingate College Library

RELIGIOUS LANGUAGE

Copyright © 1976 by Peter Donovan. Copyright under International and Pan-American Copyright Conventions. All rights reserved, including the right to reproduce this book or portions thereof in any form, except for the inclusion of brief quotations in a review. All inquiries should be addressed to Hawthorn Books, Inc., 260 Madison Avenue, New York, New York 10016. This book was manufactured in the United States of America.

Library of Congress Catalog Card Number: 75-31372

2-24-77

ISBN: 0-8015-6278-3

1 2 3 4 5 6 7 8 9 10

First published in Great Britain in 1976 by Sheldon Press, Marylebone Road, London NW1 4DU.

First published in the United States in 1976 by Hawthorn Books, Inc., 260 Madison Avenue, New York, New York 10016.

CONTENTS

069937

PHILOSOPHIZING ABOUT RELIGIOUS LANGUAGE

What is religious language? Most major religious traditions make use of more than one natural language, for their followers are drawn from different lands and talk about their faiths in their own local tongues. For some religions, however, a particular ancient language is held sacred, and used in worship even by those who do not naturally speak it. Pali, for instance, is the sacred language for Theravada Buddhists, Hebrew for Jews, and Arabic for Muslims.

But religious language, in the sense in which I shall be considering it in this book, does not mean specially sacred religious languages of antiquity. Nor does it refer to an artificial, technical language constructed by specialists in religion. There are specialists' technical terms in religious vocabularies, as there are in legal, musical, or astronautical ones. But it is not simply the presence of distinctively theological words, like 'Incarnation' or 'Apocalypse', or names of divinities, like 'Yahweh' or 'Vishnu', or titles like 'Christ' or 'Buddha', that marks out a piece of language as religious, but rather the way *any* words (often quite ordinary ones) play a role within some context of religious belief and observance.

Language becomes *religious* language in being used religiously; being used, that is to say, in the pursuit of the various goals, and the expression of the various beliefs, which we find in religions. For that reason, I shall be speaking about religious *language-use*, just as much as religious language, to show that the emphasis is less on the words themselves than on what is being done with them and in what circumstances they are occurring. 'Religious', then, rather than being taken as an adjective describing a certain kind of language, is better understood adverbially, indicating a mode or manner in which language is made to work.

1

This book is about how religious language looks, from a reflective, philosophical point of view. The subject called Philosophy of Religion is an important member of that group of modern ways of approaching religions commonly called Religious Studies. Philosophers of religion are particularly interested in religious language, since many of them are indebted to the methods and discipline of modern *linguistic* philosophy—so much so, that there have been criticisms of contemporary philosophy for confining itself to 'talking about talk', and neglecting the obvious fact that there is a great deal more to a subject like religion than simply words. As Ninian Smart reminds us:

> the philosophy of religion is essentially about *religion*, and religion as we find it has to do with prayers and incense and the numinous and worship and practical conduct. Religion as we find it is embedded in rites, and yoga, and meditation, and churches, and temples, and monasteries, and music, and art.[1]

Yet despite the fact that words form only a part of the whole business of religious life and faith, it is important to keep in mind just how much language does for religion. Languages, systems of communication, ways of expressing things and reflecting upon them, give religious experience continuing points of contact with wider human experience and knowledge. Without a medium such as language, religion would be largely a private affair, harder to share even than aesthetic experience or deep emotion. There may well be an inexpressible side to religion, and there certainly is much more to religious behaviour than the uttering of words, yet language is essential for religions to have a form that can survive, transmit itself from one age to another, spread from place to place, and permeate human thinking and action. Furthermore, words reflect *content*. Religious believers typically assume that they have knowledge, insight, or information not possessed by those who do not hold their beliefs. It is what they can tell others and what they can say for themselves that will show, if anything can, whether their assumptions can be borne out. There are indeed ways of impressing others with the validity of one's beliefs besides telling them things. But it is with the truth or falsity of what religions teach, the reliability

[1] Ninian Smart, *Philosophy of Religion* (Random House 1970), p. 26.

2

or deceptiveness of the claims they make for themselves, that the questioner about religion will be chiefly concerned.

Most modern approaches to the study of religions emphasize the need for sympathetic appreciation, rather than criticism or the passing of judgement on the beliefs and practices of the religious system under study. 'Withhold judgement', the phenomenologist of religion tells us. 'Try to see and feel what it means to participate in those beliefs and ways of speaking as an insider, a believer to whom the realities spoken of are real, and for whom the claims made are true.' There is clearly much to be said for this approach, as a guard against superficial, polemical discussions of religious beliefs, without any appreciation of their depth and complexity.

A philosopher, however, looking at religious language-use, may well have an uneasy conscience about too readily letting himself appreciate it, on its own terms, in an affirmative and uncritical way. For while it may be endlessly satisfying and absorbing to study the rich complexity of people's language-use, its subtle connections with their cultures and their behaviour, and so on, one question comes continually to the philosopher's mind: 'Are people being misled by all this?' For he knows, from his general philosophical experience, how blind people can be to the confusions of their own ways of talking, how ignorant of the lack of basis for many of their fundamental commitments. He remembers that philosophers themselves are commonly deceived and led astray by their own language-use. He can never be sure he will not be forced, in examining religion, like the child in the story of The Emperor's New Clothes, to speak out and say what others are refusing to see.

Nor should those who study religion in other ways, historians, theologians, phenomenologists, sociologists and anthropologists, for instance, object to philosophers wanting the right to ask critical questions about religions and their uses of language. (They may, of course, rightly complain if the questions are being asked and answered too hastily, without a full enough consideration of the subject.) But if they do *not* care one way or the other whether religious language misleads people, arouses false hopes, or inaccurately represents reality, they are scarcely being true to their own principles of taking religions as they find them. For there is little doubt that religious people themselves *do* care that their words be taken as the truth, and would be offended at the suggestion that it did not matter whether their language was misleading and their claims dishonest. For they attempt to convert others by proclaiming their beliefs as facts; they argue against heresies and other religions, denouncing them as lies or distortions; they may even accept ostracism and death, rather than admit that they could be wrong.

The philosopher of religion is not, then, making an unfounded assumption, when he proceeds as though there really were questions about validity, intelligibility, plausibility and truth, to be asked of religious language. For questions like those *are* relevant, in the study of religions, however difficult it may be to frame them appropriately, let alone to begin to answer them.

For the reasons just given, then, this book will confine its attention mostly to the peculiar philosophical problems associated with religious *claims*, i.e., utterances or statements which appear to assert that certain states of affairs are so, certain things are the case. While many of the other features of religious language will be considered along the way, it is to the truth-claiming uses of language I shall constantly return. For unless he can feel reasonably sure he understands the nature of these, the philosopher, and perhaps most reflective people with him, will hesitate before being too greatly impressed by other features of the language and literature of religions.

There are many important things about religious language which I shall not discuss: the growth and development of its technical vocabularies, questions about translating and interpreting sacred scriptures, the influence of religion on secular language and literature, how to communicate traditional doctrines to modern man, and so on. Readers must look elsewhere for discussions of those topics. Yet even though this book says nothing directly about them, its discussion of the truth-claiming, assertion-making side of religious language-use cannot help but have indirect relevance to most of its other aspects. For an introduction to philosophizing about religious language, the topics chosen here are unquestionably among the most important.

Some readers may feel that a disproportionate number of examples and illustrations are drawn from the Christian religion. Since most discussions in recent philosophy of religion use predominantly Judaeo–Christian materials for their subject-matter,

4

it is inevitable that a greater amount of material from that source should occupy our attention. Other religious writings will be mentioned too, however, from time to time. I believe that there are sufficient common problems about language-use in all religions for a discussion of examples drawn from any of them to throw light on the others.

References to other books have for the most part been confined to works highly relevant to the subjects under discussion. For background reading and further study, it is suggested that the books and journal articles from which quotations are drawn or which are otherwise mentioned be treated as a basic bibliography. For convenience, the most important of these are listed at the end of the book. More advanced bibliographies for modern philosophy of religion may be found in Basil Mitchell, ed., *The Philosophy of Religion*. Oxford University Press 1971; and Terence Penelhum, *Problems of Religious Knowledge*. Macmillan 1971.

1

SEEING THE DIFFICULTY IN RELIGIOUS STATEMENTS

When we study religions we find ourselves having to learn many new words. We are expected to follow the reasoning of some very obscure arguments. We are faced with long lists of rules, precepts, and catalogues of sins and virtues. Confusingly similar foreign names have to be distinguished from one another. And, above all, we have to make the effort to appreciate the meaning of a great number of extraordinary stories and out-of-this-world claims, often expressed with elaborate rhetoric or devotional sentiment. Yet new terms and concepts do not in themselves pose a serious problem. People pick them up easily enough when learning astronomy or botany, assembling electronic equipment, or experimenting with exotic cookery. Complicated sets of rules, too, are mastered by us all without very much effort: the Highway Code, for instance, or the rules of games. And we are all used to extraordinary stories and a good bit of rhetoric and sentiment, brought to us each day by the news and entertainment media. What, then, is the special problem about religious language? Why single it out, as a *philosophical* issue?

Is the difficulty which philosophically-minded people seem to find in religious language simply a matter of unfamiliarity—the sense of strangeness felt by an outsider or newcomer? If that were so, then the problems would not be fundamental, and could be overcome with time. The insecure feeling of 'not being sure what is going on' we all experience in the first few days of a new job has vanished completely after six months or a year. Perhaps the philosopher who looks at religions is likewise a 'new boy', who can't be expected to make sense of everything at first.

To regular users of religious language, believers who sing and pray, listen to sermons, recite creeds, and read sacred books, the language of religion can indeed seem almost as familiar and straightforward as that which they read in the daily newspaper. But once questions are raised: 'Just what do you mean by... ?', 'In what *sense*... ?', 'Is it *literally* true that. .. ?', the oddness of the language-use becomes more obvious, and the sense of familiarity begins to vanish, even for the insider.

On the face of it, such well-loved Christian writings as the twenty-third Psalm or the Lord's Prayer are as clear and simple as can be. But their meaning turns out to be far from obvious when the attempt is made to say just what, in ordinary day-to-day terms, they come to. 'Our Father' (though not our parent), 'Who art in heaven' (though not amongst the stars) ..., 'give us this day our daily bread' (which we will have to buy) ..., 'deliver us from evil' (does that mean accidents and illness too?). The words themselves are clear enough, but what do they really tell us? What do they add up to? One observer of religious language has put the problem this way:

> Suppose I am told of a new theological discovery, namely that Brahma wears a hat. And then I am told that it is a divine hat and worn infinitely, since Brahma has neither head nor shape. In what sense then is a hat being worn? Why use *these* words? I am told that God exists but in a 'different sense' of *exists*. Then if he doesn't exist (in the plain sense) why use *that* word? Or that God loves us—but in a wholly special sense of *love*. Or God is a circle whose centre is everywhere and circumference nowhere. But this is then to have neither a centre nor a circumference, and hence not to be a circle. One half of the description cancels out the other half. And what is left over but just noise?[1]

IS RELIGIOUS LANGUAGE ALL FIGURATIVE?

Perhaps the problem is just a failure to recognize how much religious language is figurative or symbolic. The literature of the religions of the world is remarkably rich with figurative uses

---

[1] Arthur C. Danto, 'Faith, Language, and Religious Experience. A Dialogue', in *Religious Experience and Truth*, Sidney Hook, ed. (Oliver and Boyd 1962), p. 147.

of language. Much of the pleasure of learning about religions comes from the fine examples of imaginative literary forms they have to offer, whether they be myths and legends of the Ancient Near East, Greece, or Polynesia, the epics of India, the epigrams and proverbs of Confucius and the Wisdom books, parables of the Gospels or Jataka tales, or the clever analogies of Sufi theologians and Buddhist 'Questions of King Milinda'. But it is too simple a view to think that all the difficulties people find in, say, the language of Christianity, would disappear if only they were to add 'not literally, of course' to every Christian statement or utterance.

Certainly many of the usual terms applied to Jesus and God in Christianity are intended and generally taken as non-literal or in some sense figurative. God speaks, listens, acts, draws near ... Jesus came from above, ascended to the right hand of God, and will return to judge the living and the dead. The words are common, earthly words, but put to a special, out-of-the-ordinary use. We know what speaking, listening, acting mean, when referring to someone with a body. But God has no body. We understand that men come from, ascend to, or return from various places—but places located somewhere in space. When these things are said of God and Jesus the situation is very different from their usual use.

Yet not all Christian statements are of this secondhand kind, derived from ordinary use yet very different from it. Some, for instance, are simply records of historical incidents:

> When the day of Pentecost had come, they were all together in one place. Acts 2.1

Some tell of unusual occurrences:

> And suddenly a sound came from heaven like the rush of a mighty wind, and it filled all the house where they were sitting. Acts 2.2

Some relate peculiar experiences:

> And there appeared to them tongues as of fire, distributed and resting on each of them. Acts 2.3

And some go on to describe those occurrences and experiences,

8

and say what they are supposed to mean, using distinctively religious terms:

> And they were all filled with the Holy Spirit and began to speak in other tongues, as the Spirit gave them utterance.
>
> Acts 2.4

There we have in four short verses a range of quite distinct uses of language in a religious context, to which no simple distinction between literal and figurative can be readily applied. Thus it is just not true that Christian language is all figurative. Many of the key words in religious statements, as Ninian Smart has pointed out, so far from being used figuratively in religion and literally elsewhere, are used literally in religion and figuratively elsewhere.

> When I say 'God is holy', I am using 'God' and 'holy' literally, but when I say that Mao Tse-tung is the god of the Chinese, I am using 'god' analogically; and when I say that my son is a 'holy terror', I am not using 'holy' literally. There are lots of other examples—sacrament, sacrifice, prayer, amen, spiritual, divinity, numen, grace, eternal, hallowed, etc.[2]

Religious language is not only made up of language borrowed from other sources and used in figurative ways; some of it is original and underived.

FIGURATIVE LANGUAGE GIVES US A CLUE TO THE PROBLEM

Although it is a mistake to assume that all religious language is a type of figurative language, there are features of the figurative use of language which can give us clues to seeing the particular philosophical problem raised by religious statements. Figurative language is commonly affective language—that is to say, it affects people's feelings, enters into their imagination, and influences their emotions. So, too, does much religious language. Its symbolism and poetry give it power to evoke a sense of the profound and the sublime, to speak to the heart. Religion is thereby prevented from being a merely intellectual exercise. It is

[2] *The Philosophy of Religion* (Random House 1970), pp. 66-7.

9

kept in touch with man's emotional responses and his moral and aesthetic sensitivities.

Philosophy, in investigating religion, has no objection to profound feelings or depth of human emotion. Yet the very affective power which religion shows in its poetic forms of language, philosophy recognizes as the thing about it most likely to mislead. The reason for that can be explained as follows: There are two quite different reasons why religions tend to speak in oblique, indirect ways.

First, they are attempting to express deep experiences and emotions and to influence human response and behaviour. Secondly, they are attempting to talk about an elusive and obscure subject-matter (whether that be a god or gods, supernatural states of affairs, or mystical levels of consciousness). Oblique, figurative language lends itself to the former aim, the arousing of human response. And it can hardly be avoided for the latter, the attempt to speak about the transcendent. The danger is that by succeeding in its first aim religious language can too easily create the impression that the second aim also has been achieved.

The effectiveness of an apt simile, for instance, a subtle blend of images, or a cleverly-drawn parable, can seem like the dawning of some profound truth about reality. Consider, for instance, this typical Buddhist parable:

It easily happens that a man, when taking a bath, steps upon a wet rope and imagines that it is a snake. Horror will overcome him, and he will shake from fear, anticipating in his mind all the agonies caused by the serpent's venomous bite. What a relief does this man experience when he sees that the rope is no snake. The cause of his fright lies in his error, his illusion. If the true nature of the rope is recognized, his tranquillity of mind will come back to him; he will feel relieved; he will be joyful and happy. This is the state of mind of one who has recognized that there is no self, that the cause of all his troubles, cares, and vanities is a mirage, a shadow, a dream.[3]

[3] Part of the Buddha's 'Sermon at Benares', from the *Mahavaggha*. This extract from *World of the Buddha: A Reader*, Lucien Stryk. ed. (Doubleday, Anchor Books edition, 1969), p. 52.

The parable is clearly a good one, effectively expressing the Buddha's message that release comes through recognizing the self to be an illusion. Yet the parable would mislead, and the state of mind it urges be ill-advised, if there *were* nonetheless an immortal self to be concerned about. The truth or falsity of the claim being asserted, in other words, depends not at all on the effectiveness of the parable, but on whether it represents what is in fact the case. The same is true of the Gospel parables about the 'Kingdom of God'. They enlighten us as to what the kingly rule of God is thought by Jesus to be like. But they do nothing at all, in themselves, to establish that there is such a thing, even though they would be quite unjustified if there were not.[4]

Not every meaningful use of language, however much it seems to 'ring true' or illuminate us, has a basis in reality. As Ronald Hepburn reminds us, 'After composing the most tightly coherent sonnet to his beloved, the poet may discover that his love for her wanes and that he no longer can "apply" the poem to her.'[5] Like words in poems, words used in religious statements *seem* to have a sense. They follow rules of grammar, create images and arouse emotions, and often give the impression of conveying profound truth. But used as they are obliquely, outside reliable, everyday contexts, what safeguards are there against their being simply poetic flights of fancy with no basis in fact?

EVOCATIVE AND INFORMATIVE USES OF LANGUAGE

To make clearer the problems raised by oblique uses of language, a distinction can be drawn between the *evocative* power of an expression (what it brings to mind) and its *informative* content (what information it in fact communicates). It is obvious that many expressions are both evocative and informative, e.g., a roadside 'Hot Meals' sign to a hungry motorist. Very few expressions are completely lacking in evocative power, since almost any word or sign can call up associations in our minds,

---

[4] The fact that the parables in those examples are first told by someone taken to be an authority on the subject is, of course, an important, but different, consideration. See below, Chapter 6.

[5] 'Poetry and Religious Belief', in *Metaphysical Beliefs*, Alasdair MacIntyre, ed. (S.C.M. Press 1957), p. 87.

even though totally uninformative. But not every expression is informative, and some that appear to be may let us down. (The 'Hot Meals' sign may simply have fallen from a sign-writer's van, or the hungry driver may have unconsciously day-dreamed it, in his mind's eye.)

The evocative side of religious language, symbolism and imagery provides material for a variety of studies, from literary criticism to psychoanalysis. Much work has been done on the origins and development of religious symbols, and their places in human worship and culture.[6] But for philosophical purposes, how a given symbol or expression comes to have the power to bring certain things to mind is of no particular importance. Philosophy takes for granted that, for many different reasons, religious words can be evocative, often powerfully so. It is more concerned with whether religious statements genuinely *tell us something*, along with the images they evoke and the part they play in affecting human behaviour and response.

OBLIQUE STATEMENTS MAY STILL BE INFORMATIVE

When, then, are statements in oblique, figurative terms reliable, and when do they mislead? Figurativeness does not in itself, of course, prevent informativeness. As guides to good writing tell us, figures of speech can often communicate information more efficiently than their literal alternatives ('His face fell', for 'he suddenly showed disappointment', and so on). Yet a suspicion remains that when figurative, oblique expressions are used, what is being said is poetic and somehow not quite accurate. On the other hand, when the word *literally* is used, the emphasis is on the exactness of the terms in which some description is given ('He was literally down to his last dollar').

We might expect, then, that a closer look at the difference between *literal* and *figurative* statements will help us better to appreciate the difficulty in religious statements. But there is no simple formula by which to distinguish literal from figurative uses. Much depends upon their context and the intention of the

[6] See, for example, Edwyn Bevan, *Symbolism and Belief*, 1938, re-published Fontana 1962; F. W. Dillistone, *Christianity and Symbolism*. Collins 1955; T. Fawcett, *The Symbolic Language of Religion*. S.C.M. Press 1970; John Macquarrie, *God-Talk*. S.C.M. Press 1967

users. Everyday language is full of uses which have figurative origins and overtones; not only conscious ones like 'having a whale of a time', and almost unnoticed ones like 'seeing the point of a joke'—but extended uses which have become quite unnoticed, like 'broadcasting' for radio transmission, and 'vacation' for holiday trip. If by *literal* we mean language in which no stretched or borrowed meanings occur, then very little of our everyday language is literal at all.

Most figurative language we come across has been purposely chosen for its evocative, poetic or expressive power. It is not the basic currency of communication, but it can be cashed on demand, so to speak, into something less figurative, though with some loss of effectiveness. In contexts where, above all, factual accuracy is called for (law reports, technical descriptions, or medical diagnoses, for instance), direct rather than oblique, figurative language is generally insisted upon. For such subjects non-figurative speech is more reliable; it is, as we put it, 'the literal truth', the informative rather than the evocative side of language, that the lawyer, the technician, or the doctor is interested in.

Perhaps the best sense that can be given to the distinction between literal and figurative language then is this: the less figurative a statement, the less reflecting on it we must do, before we can extract the information it contains and check its credentials. With very obscure figures that process can hardly even begin. If you tell me, for instance, that your car is a well-kept, mechanically sound 1965 Mini, the information I gain from your statement is easily checked. If you describe it as a 'trusty steed', again, since the figure of speech is well known, I have little difficulty in following your meaning, and can easily work out for myself what observations to make to check the truth of the description. But suppose you use a totally unfamiliar figure, likening the car to, say, a dragonfly. What reliable information can I gain from the various images that simile evokes? Is the car flimsy and fragile? or amphibious? or inclined to dart hither and thither...? Despite what I know about cars and dragonflies, I cannot tell whether I am getting the point of what you intended to convey to me. The best I can do is to ask you to tell me more, or to put your description less figuratively.

The difficulty of oblique language, then, is that before we

13

Wingate College Library.

can decide whether it is misleading or not, we may have to do some further work on it. In the case of figurative statements in ordinary language we can usually ask for further information or think up an appropriate translation into terms we can more easily check or appraise. But with the oblique statements so typical of religions there often seem to be no alternative expressions which are better known to us and thus more easily tested for informativeness. No matter how much we ask for further information, what we are told is still expressed in analogies, parables, metaphors or symbols—all oblique forms of expression, with no clear criteria by which to check their reliability.

WHY INFORMATIVENESS IS IMPORTANT FOR RELIGIOUS STATEMENTS

If nothing much turns on it, we may not be very concerned that some pieces of language seem incurably oblique and obscure. But once the question of their informativeness is seen as a crucial issue it is a different matter. Think how quickly arguments arise over whether some vague remark was intended as a compliment or an insult; or how important it can be to decide whether the babbling of a distressed child is an attempt to tell us something we ought to know. In its oblique and evocative character, much religious language resembles poetry. But unlike most poetry, religious utterances commonly claim to convey information of unique significance, the understanding of which may be of supreme importance for its hearers. It is that possibility, together with the alternative possibility that vast numbers of people are grossly misled by religion, that gives urgency to the philosophical task of investigating religious language-use.

2

AVOIDING EMPTY TALK

There are times when empty talk is quite harmless. Entertainers make their living out of it. Parents put their children to sleep with it. Most people use it a good deal, in everyday social life. But in more serious affairs we have nowadays a dislike for empty words. We ignore Special Offers which amount to nothing; we switch off political broadcasts when they become mere oratory; we tear up and throw away guarantees and warranties which so commonly are, as we say, 'not worth the paper they are printed on'. Much of our suspicion of words is the result of harsh experience. We have too often been taken in by statements which we accepted at face value, only to find our hopes and expectations unfulfilled when they turn out to be lies or exaggerations.

The best philosophers have always been aware of the power of words to deceive, by seeming to be full of meaning yet signifying nothing. Plato, for instance, warns his readers that the poet or the dramatist:

> ... can use words as a medium to paint a picture of any craftsman, though he knows nothing except how to represent him, and the metre and rhythm and music will persuade people who are as ignorant as he is, and who judge merely from his words, that he really has something to say about shoemaking or generalship or whatever it may be. So great is the natural magic of poetry. Strip it of its poetic colouring, reduce it to plain prose, and I think you know how little it amounts to.[1]

Wittgenstein speaks for modern philosophy, similarly, when he claims that 'the confusions which occupy us arise when language is like an engine idling, not when it is doing work'. Philosophical

[1] *The Republic*, Book X, H. D. P. Lee, tr. (Penguin 1955), p. 377.

problems, he suggests, arise 'when language goes on holiday'.[2]

EMPIRICISM AS A SAFEGUARD AGAINST EMPTY TALK

The movement in philosophy known as *empiricism*, especially in its modern form of linguistic empiricism, has concerned itself particularly with finding ways to avoid empty claims and vacuous assertions. In 1936 A. J. Ayer published what was to become a widely-influential book *Language, Truth and Logic*, in a bold attempt to show how philosophy could get rid of the nonsense of empty talk. He claims the eighteenth-century philosopher Hume as his ally, and quotes a memorable Humean passage:

> If [says Hume] we take in our hand any volume; of divinity, or school metaphysics, for instance; let us ask, Does it contain any abstract reasoning concerning quantity or number? No. Does it contain any experimental reasoning concerning matter of fact and existence? No. Commit it then to the flames. For it can contain nothing but sophistry and illusion.[3]

'What is this', Ayer observes, 'but a rhetorical version of our own thesis that a sentence which does not express either a formally true proposition [like a proposition of arithmetic or deductive logic] or an empirical hypothesis [a claim based on observations of the world around us] is devoid of literal significance.'[4]

Empiricists like Ayer, then, consider it to be a very reasonable safeguard, in philosophy, to take as a standard the ways in which we talk about the material world as we know it through observation by our senses. This is the place where we learn informative language, and in which we first come across distinctions between meaningful and meaningless, true and false, informative and empty. If we can find what it is about this kind of talk which gives it its reliability, then we will have a principle by which to assess other more difficult kinds of discourse.

[2] *Philosophical Investigations*, G. E. M. Anscombe, tr. (Blackwell 1958), pars. 132, 38.
[3] *Language, Truth and Logic* (2nd edn Gollancz 1946), p. 54.
[4] *Ibid.*

Empiricism as a total philosophical position has its critics.[5] But there is no doubt that the success of empirical ways of discovering knowledge, and the commonsense procedure of learning by experience, make it a sensible approach to adopt. Putting to the test of investigation through the senses is, after all, our most usual way of distinguishing what is the case from what is not.

Much discussion in recent philosophy of religion has stemmed from applying a similar standard to religious language as a means of finding whether it is empty talk, or whether it may have informative content. An empiricist approach to religious claims goes like this:

> ... whatever it is that we are allegedly asserting if we are making a genuine factual assertion, it must be possible to show what it would be like for the assertion to be true or probably true and what it would be like for the assertion to be false or probably false. If that condition did not obtain, if God-talk does not lay itself open to experiential confirmation or disconfirmation in this way ... it, no matter how emotively meaningful, is without factual significance and makes no genuine truth-claim.[6]

How well can religious language measure up to such a standard?

FLEW'S CHALLENGE

An interesting and fruitful debate on that question in recent years has centred on a short paper by Antony Flew, published as part of a discussion entitled 'Theology and Falsification'.[7] Flew's empiricist approach maintains that for a statement to be factually informative (cognitively meaningful) there must be

[5] See, for instance, H. D. Lewis, *Philosophy of Religion* (English Universities Press 1965), chapter 13, and further reading mentioned there.

[6] Kai Nielsen, *Contemporary Critiques of Religion* (Macmillan 1971), p. 40.

[7] Published with other related papers in *New Essays in Philosophical Theology*, Antony Flew and Alasdair MacIntyre eds (S.C.M. Press 1955) and quoted here from *Philosophy of Religion*, Basil Mitchell ed. (Oxford University Press 1971), pp. 13-15.

some empirically discoverable state of affairs at least conceivable which would count against that statement, i.e., tend to show it false. Testing for informativeness is here being treated as a matter of falsifying (showing false) rather than verifying (showing true), since what counts conclusively *against* some very general proposition may often be easier to specify than what counts for it. As Flew puts it:

> Suppose ... we are in doubt as to what someone who gives vent to an utterance is asserting, or suppose that, more radically, we are sceptical as to whether he is really asserting anything at all, one way of trying to understand (or perhaps it will be to expose) his utterance is to attempt to find what he would regard as counting against or as being incompatible with, its truth.[8]

Flew has already pointed out the tendency of religious believers continually to shift their ground, to qualify their claims so as to avoid apparent falsification by the evidence. He illustrates this 'death by a thousand qualifications' with the story of a mysterious gardener. Such a being is held by an explorer to be tending a plot of jungle vaguely resembling a garden. Despite the failure of all known tests to detect any gardener, the explorer persists in his claim, continually qualifying it to avoid admitting that the tests count against it. The gardener, he explains, makes no sound, cannot be seen, leaves no footprints, and so on. His fellow-explorer is left wondering how such an invisible, intangible, imperceptible ... etc. gardener differs from no gardener at all. What seemed to have been a statement of fact, 'some gardener tends this plot', now appears to be simply a picturesque way of talking about the jungle, perhaps a way of drawing attention to its garden-like features, but not an informative, factual statement about anything other than the jungle at all.

Flew's mysterious gardener story (first told by John Wisdom) reminds us of A. A. Milne's *House at Pooh Corner*, and the occasion when Tigger, a newcomer to the forest, descends on Pooh unexpectedly at midnight.[9]

[8] *Ibid.*, p. 14.
[9] A. A. Milne, *The House at Pooh Corner* (Methuen 1928), chapter 2.

'Well', said Pooh, 'it's the middle of the night, which is a good time for going to sleep. And tomorrow morning we'll have some honey for breakfast. Do Tiggers like honey?'
'They like everything', said Tigger cheerfully.

Next morning, however, after trying some honey, Tigger is forced to admit

'Tiggers don't like honey.'
'Oh!' said Pooh, and tried to make it sound Sad and Regretful.
'I thought they liked everything.'
'Everything except honey', said Tigger.

They then try 'haycorns' at Piglet's; and again Tigger qualifies his original assertion.

'Tiggers don't like haycorns.'
'But you said they liked everything except honey', said Pooh.
'Everything except honey *and* haycorns', explained Tigger.

A further attempt to satisfy Tigger, this time with thistles at Eeyore's, also fails.

'But you said', began Pooh, '—you *said* that Tiggers liked everything except honey and haycorns.'
'*And* thistles', said Tigger, who was now running round in circles with his tongue hanging out.

Fortunately Tigger finds he really *does* like the Extract of Malt which he discovers at Kanga's place. But had he continued to reject each kind of food offered him, his persistent claim 'Tiggers like everything' would have become not just false, but eventually quite pointless. What could it mean, to 'like everything, except ...' when by making endless exceptions, he has taken away from his statement all it could possibly refer to? The words have become empty.

That, suggests Flew, is the fate of many seemingly confident claims of religion. We are told, for instance, that there is a loving and powerful God, or that the Creator of the universe is Sovereign Lord of all things, yet when religious believers are confronted with apparent evidence against such claims (suffering, famine, disasters, and so on), they are reluctant to admit the force of the evidence, and instead produce qualifications of their original assertions. ('Divine love is beyond human under-standing'; 'God's power is manifested in spiritual rather than material ways'; and so on.)

But if believers refuse to admit that *any* state of affairs known or conceivable, in human experience, would have to be admitted as counting against assertions like 'God is good and powerful', then that claim itself, however much it may appear to be a state-ment of fact, does not convey any information at all. What it appears to say is not just not true—it is empty, or, as Flew puts it, cognitively meaningless. Statements which fail to pay the necessary price for factuality (i.e., being open to confirming or falsifying observations) cannot be counted as statements of fact.

Notice that Flew is not saying religious statements are totally meaningless or nonsensical. He recognizes that they can be full of poetic meaning at times, evocative of much imagery, and even suggestive of many *possible* factual meanings—on the face of them at least. He accepts that talk about God being 'loving', 'like a father' and so on, might express meaningful analogies and have genuine applications to experienceable facts. He simply finds that once he follows up the lines of investigation suggested by the analogies for testing their informativeness, his negative findings are rejected by those who make the claims; yet they in turn refuse to specify what observations and tests would count against the claims being true. He concludes then that the statements are not factual after all, but remain vacuous and uninformative.

Some defenders of religion may object, 'Why should religious statements be expected to meet standards proposed by philoso-phers—sceptical ones at that?' Puzzlement and doubt about the factuality of religious claims is not, however, something which has only recently been invented by philosophers. It is a wide-spread feature of modern, secularized thought—the suspicion that traditional supernaturalistic religious talk is largely empty, or at least that it has not had the function those who have used it took it to have, namely, giving information about realities beyond this present, perceptible world. Philosophers like Ayer, Nielsen and Flew know how to express these doubts clearly and can show more precisely just where the problems are in religious claims. But they are problems which everybody, not just philoso-phers, can sense.

Another possible objection is to point out that Flew and other empiricists seem to be insisting that God, if he is to be known at all, must be experienced in much the same way as ordinary things like tables and chairs; i.e., through making a difference to things discernible by the human senses. But that is surely bringing the Creator down to the level of his creation, treating him as one thing among others, instead of as First Cause and Ground of all existing things. The infinite God is far beyond the limitations of finite human perception; he cannot be observed with our feeble senses.

As a religious reaction to empiricism that objection is quite understandable. But it amounts to what in law courts is called 'special pleading'; that is to say, it tries to show that language used of God or other supernatural realities should be 'let off lightly', since, being unique, these things can hardly be expected to meet the same kinds of conditions as talk about more ordinary subject-matter. The difficulty with special pleading on behalf of religious language is that it tends to beg the question. It is all very well to appeal, as is often done, to Aristotle's maxim that 'an educated man looks for precision in things only so far as the nature of the subject-matter admits'. But to use that as an excuse for religious language still implies that one can say *something* about the subject-matter, namely, the kinds of things that have to be said if such special pleading is to carry any weight.

There are, of course, various other quite respectable areas in which we talk about rather mysterious, non-observable things (electrons and radio waves, for instance, or other people's minds). But then there are standard sets of observations counting for or against the truth of what we say. The imperceptible electrical forces are known through the effects they have on radio receivers, oscilloscopes and cloud-chambers; the states of mind of other people are grasped through their observable behaviour and speech. Can God and the other supposed realities of religious belief also be known through their effects within human experience? That would seem to be what empiricist philosophers are asking for an assurance about, and warning us that without such an assurance the central claims of religions can hardly avoid being dismissed as meaningless and empty of factual information.

In following chapters I shall discuss some of the responses to Flew's challenge made by other philosophers of religion. The most important result of the discussion begun by Flew, however, has not been simply the suggesting of ways to defend religious assertions against the charge of meaninglessness. It has been a more careful investigation of the issues of testability, informativeness, and meaningfulness themselves.

MEANINGFULNESS, INFORMATIVENESS AND TESTABILITY

On the empiricist view, informing us about a matter of fact requires stating something not compatible with any and every observation one could possibly make. Staking out a factual claim, it is held, involves including some states of affairs and excluding others. The statement 'the animal on the mat is a cat', for instance, leads us to expect states of affairs like hearing a purring sound, observing a cat-like face with whiskers, feeling soft fur and a long tail, etc. It excludes states of affairs like feeling a scaly skin and fiery breath, observing green eyes and horns, and hearing a deafening roar. The statement 'snow is falling here' envisages states of affairs like temperatures around zero, soft flaky clusters of ice crystals fluttering to the ground, dull clouds above, etc. It excludes the states of affairs of there being a heatwave, or the speaker's being below the surface of the sea.

To put the point in general terms, if I assert some supposedly factual proposition P, you are entitled to take me to be saying something about how things will be found to be, given that P is true. If, however, I am not prepared to admit that were P *un*true anything would be found to be different, then the truth or falsity of P is no longer a live issue. For P-true seems to describe a state of affairs in no way different from P-untrue. P, in other words, does not make a factual statement after all. Whatever else it may do, it tells us nothing; that is to say, it carries no informative content. If religious claims are meant, as they usually appear, to be factually informative, then similar conditions to those just described will apply to their use. Their truth will make a testable difference to things we can in some way experience.

It is clearly a mistake, however, to take knowing-what-will-test-a-statement to be *the same as* knowing-a-statement's meaning, even if one agrees that knowing-a-statement's-meaning (if the statement is to be a factual one) includes knowing observations that will test it.

To make the meaningfulness of a statement depend entirely upon the ways of testing its truth is to overlook the point that, until some meaning is found in it, there is nothing specific enough to be tested, nothing to show what kind of test might or might not be appropriate. In other words, testability presupposes a certain amount of intelligibility. If I employ a private detective to look for clues, he must be given some idea of what the clues are to be clues to. Similarly we must understand something by the words 'God', 'loves', and the like, if we are even to begin to look for confirmatory or contrary evidence for an assertion like 'God loves mankind'. We recognize, of course, that the familiar words are put to an oblique or figurative use, when a non-observable subject such as God is involved. But it is a presupposition of all oblique uses that they bear *some* resemblance to the less oblique, more familiar uses of the terms involved.

What an oblique use of words gives us is some idea of what an assertion *might* mean. That is to say, certain possibilities are brought to mind, and to that extent the statement becomes intelligible. The question then is, what observations are available to support one possibility rather than another, or rule out connections of thought which are not intended? What features of our experience can be offered that might lead us to assert claims like those in question, or incline us to deny them? As with the example 'my car is like a dragonfly' mentioned in chapter one, when claims are made in oblique, figurative terms we can check their informativeness only if we have some idea of the things to which our attention is being drawn, and to which the truth or falsity of the claims is supposed to make a difference.

In considering possible tests or observations relevant to religious assertions, then, we are concerned not so much with putting meaning into the completely meaningless or explaining the utterly nonsensical, as with giving content to (or, if you like, substantiating) what are otherwise at best pretenders to, or candidates for, informativeness. Like wraiths in the underworld, they seem to have vague forms; but they cannot tell us anything until some empirical blood, so to speak, is put into them.

Flew's chief anxiety with religious language, an anxiety shared by empiricist philosophers in general, is to avoid the snare of empty talk, with its apparent informativeness which turns out on closer, more critical investigation, to be merely illusory. What defenders of religion are being challenged by empiricism to do, is to give a convincing account of how the utterances they make, and the kinds of thing they appear to mean by them, have any right to be taken as possible statements of fact. This is a serious challenge for the believer. For it is very difficult to think of an utterance as factually informative and worth taking seriously, when the makers of the statement themselves seem to disagree, or are hard to pin down, over what kinds of empirical happenings count for or against it. An oblique, obscure or figurative assertion may well bring to mind a number of possible factual applications, suggested by the terms of the statement itself. But for any of those possible senses to become plausible as genuinely factual and informative, some observations must be agreed to count for or against them, some tests must be accepted as relevant to their credibility.

Whether or not suitable tests *are* available for the claims of religion will be the question considered in following chapters.

3

LIVING BY RELIGIOUS STORIES

Religious believers face a challenge to admit the testability of
their claims. We saw in the last chapter that the demand is not
so much to give meaning to those claims as to give them some
substance—to show what right they have to be made as assertions of fact. Before considering the ways in which believers
might take up that challenge, we must look at an alternative
response to the demand for verification. This is the kind of response demonstrated by R. M. Hare who, in the Theology and
Falsification discussion, agreed with Flew that religious statements were factually empty as statements, but then offered an
account of their meaningfulness as what he called *bliks*, i.e.,
as principles by which one lives and in accordance with which
one interprets experience.[1]

Views like Hare's have been called *non-cognitive* accounts of
religious statements. The primary function of religious statements is not, they say, to express or convey knowledge (cog-
nition). Their meaning arises rather from some important role
or function which they play in the lives of those who use them.
R. B. Braithwaite, for instance, in *An Empiricist's View of the
Nature of Religious Belief* says that religious statements have
a meaning because they can be shown to have a use. That use
can be discovered by suitable observations, and stated in straightforward propositions. Thus, he believes, religious language can
meet the challenge of the empiricist. Religious assertions, on
this view, though non-factual, do more than simply express
emotion or evoke feelings. Braithwaite suggests that they be
regarded '. . . as being primarily declarations of adherence to a
policy of action, declarations of commitment to a way of life.'[2]

[1] See Mitchell, ed., *Philosophy of Religion* (Oxford University Press
1971), pp. 15-19.
[2] 'An Empiricist's View of the Nature of Religious Belief', re-printed
in Mitchell, ed., *Philosophy of Religion*, pp. 72-91, at p. 80.

Religious statements are expressions of intention, then, indirectly linked to a set of ideals, a policy for living, by the part they play in a religious system. Differences between religious systems themselves lie in the different sets of *stories* which are associated with their behaviour policies. As Braithwaite says:

> On the assumption that the ways of life advocated by Christianity and by Buddhism are essentially the same, [Braithwaite's own supposition] it will be the fact that the intention to follow this way of life is associated in the mind of the Christian with thinking of one set of stories (the Christian stories) while it is associated in the mind of a Buddhist with thinking of another set of stories (the Buddhist stories) which enables a Christian assertion to be distinguished from a Buddhist one.[3]

By 'story' Braithwaite means

> ... a proposition or set of propositions which are straightforwardly empirical propositions capable of empirical test and which are thought of by the religious man in connection with his resolution to follow the way of life advocated by his religion.[4]

A story is made intelligible by taking it in its most literal sense. It is not necessary, however, says Braithwaite, that the stories be true, or even that they be believed to be true. Rather, they are to be 'entertained in thought', and 'stated but not asserted'. Thus they give psychological support, and help one to carry out one's chosen way of life.

Braithwaite reminds us of the influence which Bunyan's *Pilgrim's Progress* or the novels of Dostoevsky have had on the lives of many who have been quite aware that they were fictitious. Our knowledge that the stories are not factual is neither here nor there. For the stories themselves have power to arouse certain moral attitudes and support commitment to particular behaviour policies. Braithwaite summarizes his view:

[3] *Ibid.,* p. 84.
[4] *Ibid.*

26

A religious assertion, for me, is the assertion of an intention to carry out a certain behaviour policy ... together with the implicit or explicit statement, but not the assertion, of certain stories.[5]

Not far removed from Braithwaite's view is that of T. R. Miles in *Religion and the Scientific Outlook*. Miles uses the term *parable* in a way related both to the stories of Braithwaite and the bliks of Hare. The difference between the believer and the non-believer, Miles says, '... lies in the sort of parable they tell'. Belief in God is a matter of telling the theistic parable, '... the parable of a loving father who has called us all to be like him and to become his children'.[6] Miles rules out on empiricist grounds the possibility of making meaningful statements about 'facts', 'existence', or 'reality' beyond the empirical order. He denies that we can talk sensibly about a transcendent God. At best, he offers a way of silence, but it is a silence 'qualified by parables'. As with all parables, he says, literal truth or falsity is unimportant. Their point is that they carry a message we are invited to take seriously. This, he considers, is just what religious believers do—they allow their way of life to be fundamentally affected by their accepting of the theistic parable and their living accordingly.

The non-cognitive account of religious statements illustrated by Hare, Braithwaite and Miles has had many critics, both amongst theists and non-theists alike. One chief criticism has been to object that religious assertions are not merely non-cognitively meaningful (in that they inspire and guide behaviour); they are also assumed by the great majority of those who make them, to be 'true of the way things are', to be 'in accord with reality'. And it is this assumption, above all, that gives grounds for taking them as guides for living. As John Hick says:

In order to render a distinctive style of life both attractive and rational, religious beliefs must be regarded as assertions of fact, not merely as imaginative fictions.[7]

[5] *Ibid.*, p. 89.
[6] T. R. Miles, *Religion and the Scientific Outlook* (Allen & Unwin 1957), pp. 161-2.
[7] John Hick, *Philosophy of Religion* (Prentice-Hall 1963), p. 93.

The manner in which non-cognitivists have sought to answer this criticism shows their position to be not as remote from questions of truth and fact as their critics commonly assume. Braithwaite, for instance, does not hold that one commits oneself to a way of life without any regard at all for the way things really are. On the contrary, he agrees with Hare that to the question of the choice of a way of life, every fact in the world may be relevant. Admittedly, Braithwaite says that belief in the truth of the religious stories themselves is not essential. But he does not deny that it makes sense to seek a way of life illuminated by those stories which one believes to be somehow appropriate to the way the world is.

Likewise Miles, though he denies that believers have any factual knowledge not available to unbelievers, appears to admit that some facts about the world are relevant to the decision which parables to take seriously. (For instance, he allows that the presence of evil in the world constitutes a difficulty for those who would take seriously the theistic parable.)[8] Hare, too, in his reply to Flew, makes it clear that his holding certain moral bliks (about his own continued wellbeing if he continues to live according to his lights, etc.) is linked to his having certain expectations about how things go in life.[9] There may be, in other words, factual assumptions behind the adoption of a blik, even though the blik itself is not an assertion of fact.[10]

Have Braithwaite and the others been misrepresented, then, by the use of the description *non-cognitivist*? They certainly do deny that typical religious utterances are themselves informative assertions of fact. But they appear to hold that there *is* knowledge of a sort to be gained, from the proper use of the religious stories, that the stories do, after all, have a power to get at the truth, not as direct statements of fact, but in their own oblique way.

[8] *Religion and the Scientific Outlook*, p. 171ff.
[9] In Mitchell, ed., *Philosophy of Religion*, p. 17.
[10] Paul van Buren, another non-cognitivist, has insisted that in his view questions of truth and falsity *are* involved in religious belief. The Christian pictures, he suggests, are *pragmatically* true, true 'because that is how things are': '... true because they give a leading in life which those who follow find, in an odd sort of way, to be right'. 'On Doing Theology', in *Talk of God*, G. N. A. Vesey, ed. (Macmillan 1969), p. 69.

There is, of course, a sense in which fiction can be a good guide to fact, myths and stories can contain truth, and the world of make-believe can inform us about the world of reality. Much of the interest of novels and plays, science fiction, fairy stories and so on, comes from their power to draw our attention to truths and matters of fact in the real world. They can help us to see what we too easily overlook in our observations of the things around us. (Think, for instance, of Dickens' portrayal of nineteenth-century English society in his novels, or Orwell's reminder of factual possibilities, in his fictional *1984*.)

The power of stories, parables and literal untruths to give us genuine information can be well illustrated in the case of proverbs and 'cautionary tales'. The tales of the Hare and the Tortoise, the Monkey and the Jar of Nuts, the Ass in the Lion's Skin, and many others like them, have lasted for centuries, passed from one culture to another, and still appeal today. They have survived not just because they are good entertainment, but because they each have a credible point—life is really like that. The same is true of popular proverbs, 'The early bird catches the worm', 'Too many cooks spoil the broth', 'Empty vessels make most noise'. . . . We test them, not by verification of their literal sense, but through living by them and finding them to work out in experience. Perhaps the non-literal and often paradoxical statements of religious language should be regarded in a similar way: not themselves statements of fact, but like proverbs and fables, able to teach us important truths about how life goes—able to help us see things in new ways, and thus gain a better apprehension of reality.[11]

Why should not a religious claim like 'There is a supreme being who loves all mankind', like the song 'Everybody loves somebody sometime', be taken not as a factual assertion of great generality, impossible to verify, but as a tried and tested maxim for shaping our attitude towards others, a recipe for creative human relations? Why could not 'The Lord is my Shepherd'

[11] Professor John Wisdom has reminded us, in many of his writings, of the way in which literally untrue and even absurd statements (like 'My dear, it's the Taj Mahal', said of a hat) may still be 'attempts to come at the truth'. See, for instance, 'The Logic of God', in *Paradox and Discovery* (Blackwell 1965), pp. 1-22.

function like 'Just around the corner may be sunshine for you' as an inspiration for optimistic living?

The chief objection to such an account of the meaning of religious statements is that it takes for granted a point of view called *naturalism*. The kind of information allowed to be carried by religious utterances, on such a view, is limited to what we can find for ourselves, by looking at the world and at life in the ways recommended. What they tell us, in other words, is purely about the here and now—how best to view it, how to live in it, and nothing more.

But religions, on the face of them, try to tell us much more. No one denies that they contain much practical advice about man and his natural life. But that is simply a supplement to non-natural knowledge, of more ultimate truths beyond sense experience. The most important information religions have to give, it has generally been assumed, is not about this world at all. Are all those beyond-the-natural-world claims (about God, the power of prayer, judgement, a life to come, etc.) to be taken simply as fiction, the only possible meaning of which is to help us cope better with life in this world? The reaction of most theistic thinkers to the 'living by stories' account of religious belief is well expressed in this passage from Ian Crombie:

> But success, even supreme success, in interpreting life could only confirm it as an interpretation of life. It would still be open to me, the critic may say, to admit its validity as an interpretation, but nonetheless to regard all reference contained in it to things beyond experience as simply the device by which the illumination is thrown. Is it enough, he may ask, if he admits this much?

> Of course it is not enough. The critic is not only asked to conceive of the world *as if* it were the work of a supreme intelligence, but also to believe that it *is* the work of a supreme intelligence. Creation, Redemption, Judgement are not to be accepted as illuminating fables, but affirmed as faithful parables. That these parables deepen our understanding of the world is one of the *grounds* for affirming them; it is by no means the whole content of that affirmation. To believe these doctrines is not only to believe that they illuminate the facts which come within our view, but also to believe

that they do so because they are revelatory of facts which lie outside our view.[12]

It is not enough, however, for defenders of a more traditional view of religion simply to object that non-cognitivist accounts 'leave out the supernatural'. The naturalism of those accounts arises from the conviction of the thinkers in question that where religious claims try to include 'facts which lie outside our view' they cannot meet the empiricist challenge, and so are empty. Anyone who disagrees with this conclusion is thus faced with the need to offer a better account of how other-worldly *super*naturalistic claims so characteristic of religions *can* be given substance.

IAN RAMSEY ON RELIGIOUS LANGUAGE

Readers of *Punch* will remember the regular feature which comes on the last pages of that magazine, where readers are invited to supply a caption to a cartoon taken from earlier issues. The winning effort is later published, along with the caption which appeared when the cartoon was first published (often many years before). The humour of the exercise lies in seeing how quite different captions, sometimes reflecting a complete change of mood or point of view, can make a striking difference to the way we see the picture and appreciate its point.

The way an effective caption leads us to appreciate the message of a cartoon or drawing gives us a parallel with the way religious words enable people to find meanings in the phenomena of life, with the help of imagery and concepts drawn from religious traditions. The words seem to produce a new apprehension of what is observed, bringing out otherwise unnoticed meaning and giving the observed facts an overall point.

In his book *Religious Language*[13] and in numerous other places Ian Ramsey has attempted to show that religious discourse functions in an empirically-based way, yet enables meanings of a profound and transcendent kind to be expressed. The oblique and often problematic words and phrases of religious state-

[12] 'The Possibility of Theological Statements', in *Faith and Logic*, Basil Mitchell, ed. (Allen & Unwin 1957), pp. 78-9.
[13] S.C.M. Press 1957.

ments, according to Ramsey, are admittedly 'logically odd'. But that is not a failing, for it enables them to function like the captions mentioned above. As models or stories, qualified in various ways, they are set alongside facts in such a manner as to bring about a discernment or disclosure of significance; this, where religious words are involved, leads to a peculiarly religious kind of response, a commitment of a total kind.

While religious assertions may look much like ordinary statements in form, to take them as such is to miss their distinctive characteristics, and the peculiar connection with the situations of discernment and commitment which they evoke. Ramsey produces many examples to illustrate situations where there is a discernment of *depth*, going far beyond the mere observation of matters of fact by the senses. He uses a wide range of common examples to make this point, occasions which 'come alive', in which 'the light dawns', 'the ice breaks', 'the penny drops' and so on, as the result of the use of certain words or the telling of a suitable story.

Religious language will only be understood, on this view, when it is seen in relation to the discernment and commitment situations from which it arises, and to which it continues to apply. For instance, traditional statements about God's attributes, especially the negative ones like immutability, impassibility, etc., are understood,

> if we see them as primarily evocative of what we have called the odd discernment, that characteristically religious situation which, if evoked, provokes a total commitment.[14]

Similarly with the puzzling metaphysical descriptions of God as First Cause, Almighty or Infinitely Wise, and with references to God's Eternal Purpose and to Creation *ex nihilo*. For Ramsey, theological formulae like these are to be regarded as models, qualified in certain ways so as to produce a disclosure of cosmic significance—at least that is what happens on the occasions when such terms are genuinely understood in the properly religious way, and not mistaken for straightforward assertions about a supernatural subject-matter.

At some points Ramsey sounds rather like Braithwaite who

[14] *Ibid.*, p. 50.

was discussed above, for instance, in the freedom he allows in the choice of religious expressions and stories from which discernments may come:

> ... we must recognize that while some people are impervious to some models and qualifiers, to some routes and to some stories, they may not be to others. The characteristic situation may be evoked for some by telling causal stories, for others by telling wisdom stories, for others by telling stories of good lives, for others by telling creation stories, for others by telling purpose stories. In fact there is no word which, in principle, cannot lead to a story which might evoke the characteristic situation in which God is known.[15]

But he rejects Braithwaite's limiting of the function of Christian language to the expression of commitment to an *agapeistic* way of life (Braithwaite's abbreviation for the New Testament ideal of self-giving love—from the Greek *agape*). Discussing Braithwaite's view of religious belief Ramsey objects:

> when the Christian asserts, 'God is love', he declares *primarily not* his commitment to *agape* or to an agapeistic way of life, but his commitment to certain 'facts' somehow or other described in the Gospels.[16]

He argues, against Braithwaite, that a thoroughgoing empiricism will take account not only of this-worldly experience but also of the kinds of experience to which he tries to draw attention, discernments of cosmic depth, of 'the universe and more', evoked by the religious words and stories.

Does Ramsey succeed in avoiding the naturalism implicit in Braithwaite's and Miles's accounts of religious language? It is clearly his desire to do so, and he constantly speaks as though he intends the 'disclosure of depth' to be taken as having objective content of supernatural origin. But there are some major difficulties, which critics of Ramsey's views have not been slow to point out. The difficulties arise from the attempt to treat so-called disclosure situations as providing 'empirical anchorage' for religious claims and statements. Experiences described by

[15] *Ibid.*, p. 80.
[16] In Ian T. Ramsey ed., *Christian Ethics and Contemporary Philosophy* (S.C.M. Press 1966), p. 86.

metaphors like 'the light breaking in' or 'the penny dropping' may be of considerable psychological interest. Ramsey assembles a good many examples to remind us how familiar such experiences are. But it is obvious that the mere occurrence of some disclosure-like experience is in itself no clear guide to the actual discernment of anything. A genuine discovery of information or achievement of insight may or may not be accompanied by any sudden sense of illumination or disclosure. It is easy for us to think the light has dawned, and yet to go on and show that we have got the thing completely wrong. (Anyone trying to follow a road map in a strange city will have had *that* experience.)

If the meaningfulness of oblique and figurative religious statements rests entirely on their power to lead to disclosures of profound significance, evoking total commitments, who is to be sure that heretical or blasphemous combinations of religious words, or even total nonsense, might not in some situations produce the same effect? And are the claims of religions to lose all their meaning, if it comes about that no one responds in the appropriate way to them? If that were so, they could scarcely be called truth-claims. Here our distinction in chapter one between evocative power and informative content becomes relevant. Ramsey's theory makes meaningfulness turn entirely on the evocative power of certain combinations of words. He fails to show how they can also be informative.

That is not to say that disclosures of some kind, from a transcendent source, are out of the question. Ramsey's cosmic disclosures are not unlike the kinds of mystical consciousness of higher levels of reality, supposed to be produced by paradox and negation and other meditational devices.[17] Ramsey may be correct in holding that *some* religious word-use is of that kind. His difficulty, like that of the mystics, is that if this is to be the only meaningful function of religious language, how are we to find any meaning in the language left over, so to speak, by which the supposed *content* of the mystical discernment is spelt out—attributing it, for instance, to one holy God, to whom worship is the appropriate response? A theory of the meaningfulness of religious claims, which does no more than give them the function of evoking disclosures, fails to account for the

[17] See Smart, *Philosophy of Religion* (Random House 1970), p. 43ff.

informativeness they must have for anything to be known about the object (if any) so disclosed.

Ramsey has sought to describe an empirically-anchored function for religious statements. But the sort of anchoring his theory suggests turns out, like Braithwaite's, to be largely a psychological or causal function, rather than the kind of anchoring in observable, testable matters of fact needed if the claims of religions are to count as factually informative. Admittedly Ramsey thinks religious language has far greater causal power than Braithwaite does, taking man's discernment beyond the here and now and discerning things of divine origin. But without a further account of how facts beyond the perceived world can be known and spoken about, Ramsey's account fails to answer the empiricist challenge.

Many of Ramsey's suggestions about models and qualifiers, and other non-descriptive functions of religious and theological discourse, are subtle and perceptive, and may yet be developed into a more philosophically-convincing theory. In the meantime, it is necessary to tackle the empiricist challenge head-on, and see if religious claims, taken as in some sense descriptive and cognitive, can be shown testable and open to confirming or disconfirming observations within human life and experience. The following two chapters will examine this possibility.

4

TESTING RELIGIOUS CLAIMS
IN THIS LIFE

Flew's use of the parable about the invisible gardener, and much of the discussion which follows it, assumes that so far as this present life goes there are no tests or observations which establish the truth of religious assertions. But a great majority of religious believers past and present would argue that certain tests and observations *are* relevant to religious belief, and that if carried out properly can produce evidence in support of religion's supernatural claims.

It is important to draw a distinction here between evidence and proof. Evidence is something which, if available, *tends* to prove a certain conclusion, i.e., adds weight to arguments in favour of that conclusion. A proof, however, is not just an attempt to establish a conclusion. It is a successful argument to that conclusion. It is commonly assumed that if no proof of the truth of central religious claims is available there is therefore no point in arguing them. But of course quite the opposite is the case. It is only when there *is* a proof, or a disproof, that further argument becomes irrelevant. So long as the truth of religious claims remains an open question, argument can proceed. And much of this argument will consist of drawing attention to features of the world and of the lives of people which seem to provide evidence in support of religious propositions, and weighing these against the features of life which seem to provide evidence against them. When we speak of testing the claims of religion in this life we mean, then, looking for things which might help show them to be true or false—observations to find whether they give us factual, or only fictional, information.

Testing may be a matter of simple observation. Or it may be more sophisticated, and involve the setting up of experiments and test situations. Many important things are true of the world around us which are not at all obvious from the simple evidence of our senses. Who would guess, for instance, from mere observation, that the salt we have with our meals is a combination of an explosive metal and a poisonous gas? Much of our scientific knowledge, that is to say, is the result not just of mere looking or feeling, but of the carrying out of very elaborate experiments, appropriate to the subject-matter in question, by experts who know just what to look for. Those who think religious claims are testable do not expect the evidence to be immediately obvious either. The facts in question, they say, must be approached in ways appropriate to their nature and complexity —using suitable equipment and making relevant observations. In particular, testing religious claims will involve observations connected with that very complex piece of equipment, the living human person, for it is there that the truths of religions should register, if at all.

'TRY IT AND SEE FOR YOURSELF'

In his Gifford Lectures on 'Belief', H. H. Price sums up his own attempt to offer an account of religious beliefs as follows:

I have been trying to sketch an 'Empiricist view of religion' which differs considerably from Professor Braithwaite's, one which does not part company so decisively with traditional conceptions of Theism. I have suggested that the Theistic world-outlook lays itself open at one crucial point to an empirical test. This is because an assertion about human nature is an essential part of it. The assertion is that every human being has spiritual capacities, latent in most persons and partially developed in some; and moreover that when and if these capacities are developed, or freed from the inhibitions which keep them in a latent state, experiences will be forthcoming which will support the basic Theistic propositions themselves, the propositions concerning the being and attributes of God and God's relations to us upon which the Theistic way of 'viewing the world' depends.[1]

What Price suggests there is very similar to what many religious

[1] *Belief* (Allen & Unwin 1969), pp. 487-8.

writers themselves have claimed: that to get evidence in support of the truth of religion one must approach the matter in a religiously appropriate way. This may involve cultivating a certain moral character, and developing certain spiritual capacities. Price mentions various devotional practices (e.g., prayer, meditation, and the entertaining or holding in the mind of certain scriptural narratives and religious imagery). Some such preparation, it is suggested, is essential for the would-be experimenter. In the view of Braithwaite, as we saw in the last chapter, meditating on the stories of religion draws on their power to back up one's moral commitments. Price goes further and suggests that such meditation may help develop a person's latent spiritual capacities. These may, in turn, when suitably aroused, enable the believer to obtain evidence relevant to the truth or falsity of his religion's claims. What form might that evidence take?

THE EVIDENTIAL VALUE OF RELIGIOUS EXPERIENCE

The phrase 'religious experience' is often taken to mean subjective or psychological experiences of a striking kind—visions, dreams, a sense of God's presence, the voice of conscience, the experience of grace, and the like. Religious believers have commonly thought such experiences to be strong evidence for the truth of their beliefs. And it is not unreasonable for them, as believers, to think so. For if beliefs in a personal God were true, then it would seem highly likely that certain people should have been, and be, from time to time aware of him in some way or other.

But as something to put solid factual content into religious claims, subjective religious experiences cannot on their own carry much weight. Too many alternative, naturalistic ways of interpreting them are available. So long as people can have daydreams or nightmares, or suffer from various delusions (and all these things are common enough) then it will always be open to an impartial observer to consider someone's so-called religious experience as simply an odd psychological occurrence. If it happens to loom large in the thinking and life of the person who experiences it, that is because he *reads into it* some religious significance. There will be no way of showing, by appealing simply to a subjective experience itself, whether it was what

38

it was taken to be; or only *seemed* to be. As Hobbes said, a man may tell us God has spoken to him in a dream; but if all we have to go on is his report of the experience, the most we can reasonably conclude is that he dreamt that God spoke to him.[2]

The occurrence of strikingly similar experiences amongst a sufficient number of people, all of whom have certain religious expectations, however, could be thought to raise a presumption that they were in contact with an aspect of reality not found by ordinary people in everyday experience. But as C. D. Broad once observed, large numbers of people who drink too much also seem to have strikingly similar delusions (about pink rats or snakes).[3] We do not from that fact conclude that drunkenness is a path to an unseen world, inhabited by such creatures, to which the sober are blind. Many people through training and dedication can increase their capacity to enjoy music or feel at home with abstract mathematics. The success of their efforts does not prove the real existence of higher musical or mathematical realities, to be experienced by those who approach them in the right way.

A failure to prove anything conclusively by appealing to religious experience, however, does not necessarily mean a total collapse of the argument. Suppose certain experiences *were* regularly achieved, through a method of moral and spiritual preparation of the kind H. H. Price suggests, accompanied by the earnest thinking of religious thoughts. Suppose, for instance, that the lives of those having such experiences generally changed in a direction which religions would regard as beneficial (e.g., the people became wiser, humbler, more saintly). There would then be an objective phenomenon of possible evidential value. While by no means amounting to a knock-down proof of religious claims, it is the kind of empirical observation to which the theist could well point, in taking up the empiricist's challenge.

OBJECTIVE EVIDENCES FOR RELIGIOUS TRUTH-CLAIMS

While religious experience in the subjective sense, then, has

[2] *Leviathan*, chapter 32.

[3] 'Religion, Philosophy and Psychical Research' reprinted in *God, Man and Religion*, Keith E. Yandell, ed. (McGraw-Hill 1973), p. 117.

serious limitations as evidence for religious assertions, religiously significant happenings of a more objective and public kind may well be a better kind of evidence. These include general features of the world taken as signs of the divine handiwork. (The traditional Argument from Design begins from that premise.) More especially, they include particular phenomena like miracles, providences, answered prayers, prophetic utterances and conversions. For most theistic religions these are believed to be revelatory events in which the reality and activity of God are manifested. Since such events, if they occur at all, must inevitably take place within the stream of human history, there may be a wide variety of alternative naturalistic explanations available for them. Their possible strength as evidence for religious claims comes not so much from the fact that their *occurrence* is hard to explain, but from the fact that their significance, value, or meaning is as one might expect it to be if religious beliefs were true.

Systems of religious belief offer mankind certain spiritual benefits, not only in some future life, but in the present. They speak of enlightenment, release from sin, healing of mind and body, divine guidance, etc. Suppose there actually occur in human experience events and experiences which, in certain contexts, seem to help bring about such desirable effects, and make a real difference to the spiritual quality of the lives of people who put their faith in religious systems. That would be strong evidence that belief in the systems worked—i.e., did what it claimed to be able to do.

To that the sceptic may say 'Certainly the belief works—but that does not show it is a *true* belief'. On the principle that 'a little of what you fancy does you good', even the most crazy beliefs can sometimes work wonders for those who live by them. But most religious beliefs are not known to be crazy, or even false. That is the question at issue. And once it is admitted that there do occur certain phenomena, of the kind to be expected if religious systems were valid, that fact must be allowed to count as circumstantial evidence that the beliefs on which the systems rest are true, at least to some extent (though not necessarily in all their details, since no one can be sure they have ever been adequately formulated—see below, chapter nine). If such a conclusion is ruled out, it can only be because some better explanation is available of why the systems of belief and action in question do seem to lead, in some striking cases and vast numbers of marginal ones, to something like the results they promise.

EXPERIMENTING WITH GOD

The literature of Christianity is full of the records of saints, reformers, missionaries and humble men of faith offering what they take as evidence of the particular and personal activity of God. The experiences of such people have a common pattern. They involve, very briefly, a particular commitment to a task taken to be a divine call or commission, together with the belief that the task is God's will, and that God is personally concerned to guide and protect the one taking up the task, and supply what is needed in the way of physical and spiritual resources to fulfil it. The occurrence of striking success, improbable deliverances from danger, providential provision of needs, and so on, is then quite naturally seen as evidence confirming the beliefs of the people, and a testimony to others that such beliefs are well founded.

There are even instances of outright experimentation. A good example is George Müller of Bristol, whose autobiography was widely read amongst nineteenth-century evangelical Christians in Britain and North America. Müller was distressed by the lack of deep conviction on the part of his contemporaries, so set about the specific project of establishing homes for orphans, relying simply on his belief that verses in the Bible about the providence and faithfulness of God were to be taken at face value. In his own words:

> Now, if I, a poor man, simply by prayer and faith, obtained, *without asking any individual*, the means for establishing and carrying on an Orphan-house: there would be something which, with the Lord's blessing, might be instrumental in strengthening the faith of the children of God, besides being a testimony to the consciences of the unconverted, of the reality of the things of God.[4]

[4] *A Narrative of some of The Lord's Dealings with George Müller*, written by himself. First published in 1837. 5th edn (London 1855), p. 147.

Müller was remarkably successful. Keeping throughout to his original principles (he tells us) he founded and maintained several homes and assisted many other good causes. His *Narrative* lists numbers of occasions on which needs were met, prayers answered, and helpers provided—just as though there were in fact a divine agent personally concerned with the work he was carrying on.[5]

An appropriate method for testing some of religion's claims in this life would seem, then, to be one involving the experimenter himself. For it may be that it is what happens to him, rather than what he discovers by investigation, that will be most relevant.

Austin Farrer puts the point this way:

> Is there anything in religion resembling experiment? Yes; only the person who does the experiment is God. It is God's doing, his work on us; not our doing, not our work on him. It is not, however, God's experiment; its experimental value is for us.[6]

There are, then, experiences and occurrences which seem to come about as the result of involving oneself, in various ways, in the practices and beliefs of religion—even in an experimental manner. Can religious beliefs be put to some such tests so as to produce evidence sufficient to give factual content to religious statements? Various objections can be raised to the idea of religious experimenting. Oddly enough, one of the strongest seems to come from within religion itself.

'YOU SHALL NOT PUT GOD TO THE TEST'

Several recent writers on the subject of religious language and experience appear to take very seriously the words with which Jesus rejects the devil's challenge to jump from the roof of the Temple (Matt. 4.7). On the strength of this they have ruled

[5] For one among many more recent examples of experiments in faith similar to Müller's, see Basilea Schlink, *Realities* (Oliphants 1967), the story of the Evangelical Lutheran 'Sisterhood of Mary', in Darmstadt, Germany.

[6] Austin Farrer, *A Science of God?* (Geoffrey Bles 1966), p. 95.

out the possibility of experimenting with religious beliefs.[7]

The 'heroes of faith' mentioned above, however, have been less inhibited. Perhaps they were more aware that the words of Jesus are themselves a quotation (from Deut. 6.16).[8] The words were originally applied to the Israelites tempting God out of rebellion and unbelief, and would appear to have little relevance to testing which stems from belief and faith, or even from openminded enquiry. Believers such as Müller could draw all the Biblical warrant they needed from a verse like Mal. 3.10, in which God actually invites them to put him to the test, through an act of obedience. And for the searcher prepared as Price suggests to try and see for himself, the recommendation 'Seek, and you will find; knock, and it will be opened to you' (Matt. 7.7) would similarly seem to give scriptural support, if that were felt necessary, for an experimental approach to God.

In their rejection of experiment, the writers mentioned attempt to define 'religious belief' in such a way that any sort of tentativeness or testing is ruled out. Penelhum says: 'one cannot ... take up a *belief* in order to test it.'[9] And Miles: 'If acts of commitment are carried out with some ulterior objective in mind, then, however commendable such an objective may be, the commitment is not religious.'[10] H. H. Price, however, after his thorough analysis of the idea of belief, is quite prepared to allow half-belief and less-than-total commitment as acceptable starting points in an investigation of religious claims.[11] But even if there were good grounds for ruling out an experimental frame of mind as a proper attitude for one following a religious path, there is no reason why *someone else* cannot treat the situation as a test one. The believer, if he acts according to what he believes to be divine promises or a course of action willed by God, will in fact be putting God to the test, even if that is not his intention.

[7] See, for instance, T. R. Miles, *Religious Experience* (Macmillan 1972), chapter 7; Terence Penelhum, *Religion and Rationality* (Random House 1971), p. 170.

[8] Which itself looks back to an incident recorded in Exod. 17.1–7.

[9] *Op cit.*, p. 170.

[10] *Op cit.*, p. 58 and see A. MacIntyre: '... to hold Christian belief as a hypothesis would be to render it no longer Christian belief.' 'The Logical Status of Religious Belief' in *Metaphysical Beliefs* (S.C.M. Press 1957), p. 171.

[11] See *Belief*, Series II Lecture 10.

And the test may well be one from which a religiously-informed observer can draw significant findings.

WHAT ABOUT FAILURES?

Suppose, however, that what the honest onlooker sees is the failure of events to match up to the believer's expectations? What follows then, from the tests of religious claims? There is no lack of missionaries who have died prematurely, charities that have gone bankrupt, reformations which have failed, and people whose attempts to follow divine guidance have led them wildly astray. As has often been wryly observed, records of failure are not kept with the same keenness as records of success; nor do there exist establishments with the same interest in their preservation. But the fact of failure is undeniable.

Believers themselves commonly show a persistent lack of regard for negative evidence. While this might arouse the observer's cynicism, there may be some logic in the believer's position, for negative evidence, the failure of tests, does not simply cancel out positive evidence. It will certainly make it harder for the believer's confident, general claims to be supported. But however scarce it may be, positive experimental evidence still has to be accounted for. The failure of a test does not disprove a hypothesis unless we are sure that the test was both properly carried out and entirely appropriate to the matter being tested. But in the testing of religious statements we are not in a position to be sure about either requirement. It is only when a good bit is already certain, about the subject, that we can say what will count as conclusive tests, one way or the other.

In his reply to Flew's challenge, Basil Mitchell disagreed with Flew's claim that believers do not take seriously the apparent negative evidence.

> The theologian surely would not deny that the fact of pain counts against the assertion that God loves men.... But it is true that he will not allow it—or anything—to count decisively against it; for he is committed by his faith to trust in God.[12]

[12] In Mitchell, ed., *Philosophy of Religion*, p. 18.

44

The believer, in other words, has a conscious bias, so that negative evidence does not immediately make him withdraw his claims. He is ready to accept much that happens as seeming to count against his claims, but commits himself to the hope that he will never be met with evidence that counts *conclusively* against them. He may have reasons for that hope. For instance, as Mitchell's discussion suggests, the believer may have had some experience which convinced him utterly of the rightness of his beliefs—even though he knows his report of the experience will not amount to a proof for others. Alternatively, he may be ready to meet with a good deal of contrary evidence purely on the reasonable grounds that, the possible subject-matter being what it is, ambiguity and uncertainty are only to be expected.

The analogy to be kept in mind here is not with routine laboratory demonstrating of well-known scientific laws. It is rather with investigations like psychical research, the seeking of cures for diseases, or the archaeologist's search for traces of extinct civilizations. Those engaged in such activities get their stickability not so much from a wild leap of faith, as from the quite reasonable assumption that unless someone persists, despite the likelihood of many failures and mistakes, there is little chance of any discovery being made. No doubt very few religious believers would defend on those grounds their persistence in the face of adverse experience. Yet it would be open to them to do so. And perhaps such an approach is more likely to impress observers than a believer's too eagerly accounting for all failures as a trial of his faith or as divine rebukes for unconfessed sins.

PROPORTIONING BELIEF TO THE EVIDENCE

A believer in God who appeals to religious experiences and phenomena and to the success of 'experiments with God' as evidence for the truth of religious claims has a two-stage argument to establish. He must first show that the evidence he relies on has occurred. Then he must argue that a religious interpretation of that evidence is the most convincing one.

Making quite sure that out-of-the-ordinary things have actually taken place is not as easy as it may seem. We all know from experience how unreliable can be observations made outside public, checkable conditions. The classic discussion of the point is found in the philosopher David Hume's *Essay on Miracles*. Since 'a wise man proportions his belief to the evidence', it is almost invariably more reasonable to think that incidents have been misreported or records embellished, than to accept that well-established laws of nature have been broken. Similarly with stories of extremely unlikely providential occurrences or dramatic answers to prayer, it would often seem far more sensible to think that something has been dreamed, misunderstood, or invented, than that the thing claimed has actually happened. (Exactly the same reasoning provides the basis for most people's honest doubts about ghosts, flying saucer 'sightings', or the Loch Ness monster.)

Yet strange things do happen. And sceptics overworking Hume's approach have been shown wrong time and again, once reliable methods of recording evidence had been available. The fallibility of human testimony, then, presents a problem for the tester of religious claims, but is not a complete bar to his making any progress.

Part of the difficulty with the evidence to which believers appeal is that its strikingness or wonderful relevance to their needs, prayers, or spiritual condition may be illusory. There is no doubt that having some idea in one's mind, something one is looking for, seems to give meaning or purpose to events which otherwise would be simply taken as unrelated and chance coincidences. We all know how a recently learnt word seems to crop up more frequently than we feel it did before—simply because we now have a reason for noticing it which we previously lacked. Could it be that purely psychological factors will account for the sense of 'God's wonderful intervention' both in times of crisis and in everyday affairs, which appear in devotional narratives after the style of Müller's biography and Wesley's *Journal*, or in ancient books of the acts of apostles and saints?

An objective observer, sympathetic with but not necessarily committed to the ideas of the person involved, is the best one to decide whether the impressiveness of the phenomenon is real or only illusory. Besides being sympathetic, he must also be a knowledgeable and sophisticated observer. For anything may seem a wonder or an answer to prayer if we are naive enough, or ignorant of the quite natural possibilities of life.

ALTERNATIVE NATURAL EXPLANATIONS

To make the experimental evidence for religion really strong, of course, it is not sufficient to show that some things happen which one might expect if certain religious beliefs were true. One must also show that there would not be reason to expect such things to happen, in the same circumstances, *unless* those beliefs were true. Circumstantial evidence only becomes convincing if the circumstances point to one conclusion much more strongly than to any others.

Suppose the defender of religion manages to present some very striking, well-attested evidence (miraculous healings, amazing conversions, remarkable answers to prayer, and the like). He must first meet the objection that the events are simply cases of coincidence or chance. (We all know how some very odd things can happen purely by chance.) The appeal to chance or coincidence is a way of saying 'no explanation is needed'. But using 'coincidence' in that way, to get out of having to give an explanation, can be carried only so far. Sooner or later a point may be reached at which we are not satisfied to say 'mere coincidence', and feel bound to look for a reason.

The advocate of religion may be able to show that, so far as our present knowledge goes, there are no even remotely plausible ways of accounting in natural terms for what has happened. But what is and is not remotely plausible is difficult to judge impartially. While explanation A may seem utterly implausible once we *know* explanation B to be strongly supported, so long as we are as uncertain about B as we are about A their relative merits are much harder to decide. The advocate for religion is not like the prosecutor who rules out the suggestion that fingerprints on the safe door matching those of the accused were really only a freak smudge left by the paw of a passing cat. For in that case we know already the reliability of fingerprint evidence. We cannot assume such knowledge in the case of religious phenomena. For them the question is more like whether a witness who offers an alibi for the accused really saw him where and when he says he did, or only imagined it (or did

47

neither and is lying). We cannot be sure of evaluating correctly any of the choices.

The best possible support for the religious interpretation of the facts, perhaps, would be a consensus of specialists in the very areas from which the alternative natural explanations are drawn —e.g., psychologists, physicists, or even magicians and illusionists. If they can say 'Yes, we understand the suggested natural explanation, yet see that it cannot be made convincing in this case', then the weight of the supposed evidence for a non-natural, religious claim is greatest.

It is still open for someone to insist that the failure of known natural explanations for the phenomena does not mean that there will not be discovered a natural explanation in the future. What seems a miracle in one age may be an everyday event in another. Healings, reading of minds, casting out of demons, all taken as signs of divine power in the Christian Gospels, may today be thought by many as accounted for in terms of hypnotism, telepathy, or psychotherapy. (Whether they can, or whether certain of them still differ in important ways from what those sciences can explain, is perhaps an open question. The fact that what we nowadays know as hysteria or epilepsy, for instance, might once have been regarded as spirit possession does not by itself show that spirit possession is nothing but hysteria or epilepsy. It may simply show that hysteria and epilepsy are no longer mistaken for what they are not.)

It is important for the religionist to be quite clear about just what feature of the evidence he takes to count most strongly for religious claims. It has often been argued that miracles must prove the existence of God because no natural explanations can be given of how otherwise they could come about. A stronger argument, however, is that a non-natural explanation is called for, not by the *mechanics*, so to speak, of the phenomenon (since there may simply be natural laws yet to be found which cover that) but by its qualities of purposefulness and apparent meaningfulness. In other words, it is not the 'how' of the extraordinary occurrence that is evidential, so much as its 'why', its 'as if intended' features, and its furtherance of the very things religions claim to be about.

Thus it is open to the believer both to agree that further knowledge may help explain the workings of, e.g., prayer, healing, conversion, prophecy, etc., and still to hold that when such things do work for certain religious ends, they are best seen as arising from the activity of God—since no other explanation can so well account for their appropriateness to the circumstances in which, in particular cases, they are found.

USING THE BEST EVIDENCE FIRST

The believer may think that future scientific discoveries can never endanger the evidence he relies on, since for theological reasons he holds that God can use any natural processes and events he chooses, to do his will. But the believer will be wise not to argue that way if he is to succeed in the present exercise of giving an account of how religious assertions can be shown to have unique informative content. For his claims to truth will be thoroughly unconvincing if even *he* does not appear to think they can successfully compete with natural explanations of the evidence, and override them in their explanatory power.

From the point of view of belief in God, there may be many things with thoroughly natural explanations (human love, the beauties of nature, the voice of conscience, etc.) which the believer 'receives as from God', and regards as part of the revelation of divine love and will. All those are 'evidences' of God's reality, to the believer, and form part of the content of his affirmations. But those things are not evidence in the sense of observations tending to verify, or put beyond reasonable doubt, the truths of the statements in question. For it is quite open to the non-believer, and in no way irrational for him, to see such things as fully accounted for in natural terms.

Only to the extent that believers' claims rest on phenomena *not* totally open to natural explanation can the statements they are supposed to be evidence for be regarded as giving unique factual information, and not simply presenting ordinary knowledge of natural things in a picturesque, evocative, but (so far as the non-believer can tell) thoroughly misleading way. A believer may if he likes see rainbows as a sign of God's mercy, but he needs something more than rainbows to offer us, if he is to convince us there is anything in his talk about a God who is merciful.

Again the analogy of crime detection can help. Once the crime

49

is solved, by the discovery of certain key pieces of evidence, the relevance of many other facts and details will become obvious. But it was only the key pieces that made the final solution plausible to the jury or to the public. The other pieces were useless as evidence (either because too many explanations of them were available, or because they depended too much on the subjective impressions of people involved). Similarly, it requires some good, compelling piece of evidence to make the religious case plausible. But were such evidence available, many other possible things (subjective experiences, for instance), not able on their own to carry conviction to a sceptic, would also become relevant, and able to add to an overall case.

WHOSE EVIDENCE IS TO COUNT?

One further problem about the testing of the assertions of religion must be briefly mentioned here. It is the problem of just *what* would be verified, were good evidence forthcoming of certain phenomena of a religiously significant kind.

Almost all religions have their miracle stories, their displays of supernormal powers, their prophets and their sinners-turned-saints. The Christian missionary who sets out by faith alone to take the Gospel to the ends of the earth is matched by the Muslim who leaves home, without resources, on his pilgrimage to Mecca. Both rejoice in the day-by-day care of God, and wonder at his miraculous provision for their needs. Even if there are, then, phenomena strongly inviting religious rather than natural interpretations, which to choose, amongst the available religious interpretations, is another question altogether.

Neither that question, however, nor the other difficulties discussed in this chapter, amount to a sufficient reason for rejecting the possibility of testing some central religious claims, by experiential and experimental means. What they do show is that the recommendation to 'Try it and see for yourself', even if successful in the sense of leading to religious experiences of evidential force, still leaves many issues open and many questions unanswered—in this life at least.

5

TESTING RELIGIOUS CLAIMS IN
A LIFE TO COME

The believer may be prepared to admit that as things stand no conclusive evidence in support of his claims, evidence it would be irrational to reject, can be offered to the sceptic. Perhaps we cannot, in the present life, find unambiguous clues or carry out a decisive experiment. Perhaps we simply do not see enough of the picture. But if what many religions tell us is true, then our present circumstances could change, in two important respects. First, certain predicted happenings marking the end of human history as we know it may occur; secondly, human beings may survive their bodily death and have experiences in a life to come.

THE END OF THE AGE

Judaism, Christianity and Islam, as traditionally understood, all look forward to decisive acts of God at the end of earthly history. These include the appearance on earth of a heavenly being, the Messiah or Son of Man—in Christianity, Jesus Christ himself coming to earth for a second time. Then follows a resurrection of the dead to a final judgement, and the ultimate triumph of God and his servants over all opposing powers. The end of the age is usually represented as heralded by cosmic catastrophes and earthly disorder, which will terrify unbelievers but which to believers will be conclusive signs that their final vindication and salvation are at hand.

In the Gospels, for instance, Jesus is portrayed as warning his disciples of coming persecution and strife, wars, famine and earthquakes. He then predicts:

Immediately after the tribulation of those days the sun will be darkened, and the moon will not give its light, and the stars will fall from heaven, and the powers of the heavens will be shaken; then will appear the sign of the Son of man in heaven, and then all the tribes of the earth will mourn, and they will see the Son of man coming on the clouds of heaven with power and great glory; and he will send all his angels with a loud trumpet call, and they will gather his elect from the four winds, from one end of heaven to the other.   Matt. 24.29–31

Certain Old Testament writings have a similar message (for example, Isa. 24, Dan. 7–12, Joel 2–3).

Likewise the Qur'an:

When that which is coming comes—and no soul shall then deny its coming—some shall be abased and others exalted. When the earth shakes and quivers and the mountains crumble away and scatter abroad into fine dust, you shall be divided into three multitudes; those on the right (blessed shall be those on the right!); those on the left (damned shall be those on the left!); and those to the fore (foremost shall be those!)....   (*Surah* 56, *That Which is Coming*)

Belief in decisive occurrences still to come in human history is not confined to the theistic religions mentioned. It appears even in the mythology of Buddhism, which looks ahead to a Golden Age when Maitreya, the next Buddha, will attain enlightenment and live on earth for 60,000 years, giving guidance to gods and men.

At that time, the ocean will lose much of its water and there will be much less of it than now. In consequence a world ruler will have no difficulties in passing across it. India, this island of Jambu, will be quite flat everywhere, it will measure ten thousand leagues, and all men will have the privilege of living on it. It will have innumerable inhabitants, who will commit no crimes or evil deeds, but will take pleasure in doing good.[1]

Can the sceptic deny that some such happening would be a clear verification of religious claims? Terence Penelhum has argued recently that to deny, in advance of the facts, that *any* future

[1] 'The Prophecy Concerning Maitreya', in Conze, ed., *Buddhist Scriptures* (Penguin 1969), p. 238.

happening in the world could prove theism true, is to offer an irrational and arbitrary thesis. Suppose it were to come about, for instance, that all people who let atheistic statements escape their lips were struck dumb; or that at certain times the stars in the heavens formed themselves into the words 'Praise the Lord':

> There is no good reason to think that we could not, with a little ingenuity, think up some non-theistic statements which would serve, if true, to put some theistic conclusions beyond reasonable doubt. So theistic statements are not immune to indirect proof in principle, even if the outlook for proving them in practice is completely gloomy. The facts as we know them may not be sufficient to prove them, but it is irrational to insist that nothing could.[2]

Yet the sceptic will, of course, have very good reasons for thinking that the future events relied on by the believer to support his case will never in fact happen. What is imaginable and even describable may yet be totally inconceivable as an actual happening. That is not to say that *some* of the predictions made by religious prophets about future happenings might not come true. Wars, earthquakes, famines and the like are only too frequent in human history, and thus very likely in the future. Readers of science fiction, Velikovsky's *Worlds in Collision* or von Däniken's *Chariots of the Gods?* will not find it difficult to construct in theory a cosmic catastrophe capable of producing on the earth events just like some of those foretold in the apocalyptic writings as marking the end of the age.

But being able to successfully predict the future is not in itself a proof of one's religious views of the future. The writers of the books of Daniel or Revelation may conceivably have had some precognitive awareness of future world disasters to which they gave expression in figurative and imaginative prophecies. But we can admit that prophecies may have a factual content without being forced to accept the religious interpretations the prophets themselves placed on the things they foretold. Wars and rumours of wars, plagues and strife, and even cataclysmic disasters like

[2] Terence Penelhum, *Problems of Religious Knowledge* (Macmillan 1971), p. 64.

a nuclear war could very well occur in future times, without necessarily being followed by a great unveiling of God.

Suppose, however, God were to reveal himself not merely through natural phenomena but, as the apocalyptic writers envisage, in some stupendous and supernatural way. No doubt a vision, shared by all mankind, of the opening of the sky to reveal colossal figures, thrones, radiant beings and the like can be imagined. The idea has been represented by artists and constructed by film producers. The same must also be said for the appearance on earth of a world ruler, omniscient and omnipotent, able to govern and command obedience from all nations on earth. Were such things to happen, doubt that relevant religious statements had any factual content would be finally removed.

But predictions of that kind are very different from predictions of war, disaster and cosmic chaos. These at least have some historical evidence on their side—such things have happened before and could reasonably be expected again. But out-and-out supernatural happenings for which no natural precedents can be found exist so far as we know only in the imagery of religious literature. There is not the slightest independent reason for expecting them ever to occur. The theist who defends the truth of his beliefs solely by an appeal to such utterly unexpected events is doing very little, if anything, to show that his claims are factual rather than fictional.

That there are strong differences of opinion amongst religious believers themselves about what decisive eschatological events, if any, they expect to occur, is not in itself a reason for ruling out the possibility of religious claims being verified in that way. But it does make the 'Doomsday argument', as we may call it, seem still more unimpressive to the uncommitted.

THE LIFE TO COME

There is one occurrence, however, which lack of historical precedent in itself makes no less conceivable or likely. That is the survival by a person of his death in this world, and his discovery thereafter that his religious expectations were fulfilled. Professor John Hick offers this reply to the empiricist challenge in his paper 'Theology and Verification'.[3] For Hick, the verifying or testing of statements means the removal of ignorance or uncertainty concerning their truth. He says:

What we rightly seek, when we desire the verification of a factual proposition, is not a demonstration of the logical impossibility of the proposition's being false (for this would be a self-contradictory demand), but such weight of evidence as suffices, in the type of case in question, to exclude rational doubt.[4]

The possibility of man's finding such confirming evidence, Hick points out, is built into the Christian's beliefs. For the Christian theist's picture of the universe carries with it certain expectations, not only about the end of the age or the ultimate triumph of God, but about a transformed existence for certain human beings after death—a life to come, in which doubt and uncertainty are removed.

A set of expectations based upon faith in the historical Jesus as the incarnation of God, and in his teaching as being divinely authoritative, could be so fully confirmed in *post mortem* existence as to leave no grounds for rational doubt as to the validity of that faith.[5]

Thus, suggests Hick, the demand for testability in principle can be met. Religious statements can be understood as having factual content, even though their factuality may not be substantiated except to those who survive death and experience a life to come.

DOES 'SURVIVING DEATH' MAKE SENSE?

Some have argued that there is a contradiction in the very idea of surviving death. Given our understanding of the notions *human being* and *death* it is simply nonsense to speak of a man's

[3] 'Theology and Verification', first published in *Theology Today* 17 (1960); reprinted in Basil Mitchell, ed., *Philosophy of Religion* (Oxford University Press 1971), pp. 53-71.
[4] *Ibid.*, p. 58.
[5] *Ibid.*, p. 69.

living after his death. The idea of survival, however, cannot be shown to be nonsense merely by the argument that 'we don't talk that way nowadays'. Our not talking that way may simply follow from our being ignorant about the subject; for we cannot pretend to be entirely agreed upon what we understand *human death* to be—as recent ethical and legal arguments about transplant surgery seem to show.

The more usual criticisms of Hick's appeal to the idea of surviving death point out that any mental life there might be left over, so to speak, after someone's bodily death, could not possibly count as the same person, or indeed as a person at all. What is agreed, by most writers on the subject, is that if postmortem existence is to count as anything like personal, human life, it will involve embodiment of some kind or other. For a human personality conceived of as totally disembodied would seem to lack the necessary social and communicative experiences on which the maintaining of personality depends.[6] But that conclusion, if true, is no great embarrassment to those who hold religious views of life after death. Some form of re-embodiment, whether through reincarnation, resurrection or rebirth, is by far the most generally held religious position.[7] In the theistic religions mentioned, there is felt to be no difficulty in the belief that God who has created man as a physical body, can recreate or re-embody him as circumstances require.

WOULD IT STILL BE ME?

It is not entirely clear that the appearance, in some other realm, of a being with my memory and embodied in some way resembling my earthly body, after my death, would count as *me*—and not simply as some spiritual successor of mine, whose

[6] Terence Penelhum, *Survival and Disembodied Existence* (Routledge & Kegan Paul 1970); and see H. D. Lewis, *The Self and Immortality* (Macmillan 1973) for further discussion and a bibliography of recent writings.

[7] As C. D. Broad observed: 'Of all the hundreds of millions of human beings, in every age and clime, who have believed (or have talked and acted as though they believed) in human survival, hardly any have believed in *unembodied* survival.' *Lectures in Psychical Research* (Routledge & Kegan Paul 1962), p. 408.

character is the product of my actions, thoughts, etc., during my earthly life. The same might be said, after all, of a *clone*, a human 'duplicate copy', constructed from me in this life, especially if the 'original' were to die in the cloning process. As Penelhum puts it:

> It is conceivable that there might be a future existence in which there were large numbers of persons each resembling one of us and having uncanny knowledge of our pasts. And if that world does come to be in the future, we shall not be in it. What would make it a world with us in it, rather than a world with duplicates of us in it and not ourselves? Unless we can give a clear answer to this, it seems, very paradoxically, to be a matter of arbitrary choice whether to say these future people are us or not.[8]

The arbitrariness, however, would depend very much on what went on in that world. If, for instance, there was widespread agreement amongst those present that they were survivors rather than duplicates, and if it were taken for granted by all that any rewards and punishments given there were the just deserts for lives lived in a previous earthly existence, then it would seem highly reasonable to accept that one was a survivor, and not merely a newly-minted copy. For its part in a consideration of testing religious claims in a life to come, however, the question 'would it still be me?' is not as important as might be thought. For even if a being in a future life were regarded, and regarded himself, simply as a successor of mine, that would be sufficient for religious beliefs held by me, which he remembered, to be tested. Certain of the religious beliefs I may have held, to the effect that I personally would survive death and enjoy fellowship with God, be reunited with my family, etc., would still be testable and thus factual. If what corresponded to me in the next world were not in fact me, those particular beliefs held by the earthly 'me' would have turned out to be *false*. But more general theistic beliefs could still be shown true—beliefs, for instance, about God, his creation of the universe, the exercise of his providence in worldly affairs, and so on.

Perhaps, as Penelhum seems to think, we cannot from the point of view of this life say whether identity, or merely simi-

[8] *Religion and Rationality* (Random House 1971), p. 353.

larity, would best describe the post-mortem state of affairs. But so long as that question can be decided in the next life, it does not count as a serious objection to the possibility of post-mortem verification of religious beliefs.

MERE SURVIVAL NOT ENOUGH

Mere personal survival of death, even if quite unexpected, would not necessarily convince someone without religious beliefs in his earthly life that such beliefs, which he had not held, were nonetheless true. Survival need not, in other words, fit any particular religious view. It might be, as Hick admits, simply a surprising fact, leading the sceptic to enlarge his ideas about nature and life, but still to draw no religious conclusions. Some have gone so far as to argue that *whatever* happened, in a state of post-mortem existence, would always be open to non-religious interpretation, and thus not count as conclusive evidence for the truth of religious beliefs. But on Hick's definition of verification, as the removal of rational doubt, there seems no reason to reject the possibility that, were certain things to occur in a next world, religious interpretations of the evidence would be the most reasonable available.

What sort of hereafter, we must ask, would be able to verify religious views—and not merely continue the uncertainty and ambiguity of events in our present lives? Hick describes a verifying situation as one fulfilling certain specific expectations of Christian belief. These are, first, an experience of the fulfilment of God's purpose for ourselves, as this has been disclosed in the Christian revelation; together, secondly, with an experience of communion with God as he has revealed himself in the person of Christ.

It has been objected that describing the test situation in those ways *takes for granted* the meaningfulness of religious language, such as 'the fulfilment of God's purpose', 'communion with God', 'revealed in the person of Christ' and the like.[9] Is Hick's reasoning circular? If so, his argument fails. But there is no circularity if the description of test conditions does not presuppose the factuality of the religious terms used, but simply

[9] See, for instance, Kai Nielsen, *Contemporary Critiques of Religion* (Macmillan 1971), p. 73ff.

takes them as shorthand for conditions describable, more long-windedly, in non-religious words. Basil Mitchell offers such a version of Hick's account, as follows:

> Suppose that the individual is aware of having survived death and finds himself in a situation which, if not literally identical with traditional representations of the blessed in heaven, is such that he can recognize it as what they were attempting to represent. He is in the company of men who display all the signs of intense happiness and deep mutual affection. They are in the presence of a figure who is recognizable as Jesus and they accept his authority without constraint. In him they experience an overwhelming sense of majesty and holiness of character that calls to mind, only now with far greater intensity, their moments of devotion on earth. Jesus (as on the journey to Emmaus) discloses to each of them the true meaning, as he is now able to judge, of his entire spiritual history, making clear to him how the ills he had suffered had contributed to an intelligible pattern which is now recognizably complete. Would not these experiences, taken together with others of a similar kind, which we need not specify, suffice to put the truth of traditional Christian theism beyond reasonable doubt?[10]

There may be good reasons to doubt, however, that one's first impressions, on finding oneself in a post-mortem state, would be reliable guides to how things really are. It may be appropriate, in this connection, to give some consideration to the supposed reports of communications through spiritualist mediums, or the stories told by people who have had out-of-the-body experiences. Amongst those who believe in 'spirit survival' it is a widely-held view that illusory and deceptive impressions are likely to be one's first experience after death. The contents and details of those impressions may be more likely to be determined by one's own memories, wishes and expectations than by objective realities beyond the grave.[11]

What this suggests is, of course, the need to keep in mind

[10] Basil Mitchell, *The Justification of Religious Belief* (Macmillan 1973), p. 12.
[11] See C. D. Broad, *op. cit.*, Section C.

the possibility that one may be *mistaken* in a post-mortem life. The point is dramatically illustrated in the practice of Tibetan Buddhism. There the *Book of the Dead* is read by a lama to the dying person. It contains a precise picture of what he can expect in the next world and how to turn to his advantage the things that he will experience there.

> Three and a half days after your death, Buddhas and Bodhisattvas will for seven days appear to you in their benign and peaceful aspect. Their light will shine upon you, but it will be so radiant that you will scarcely be able to look at it. Wonderful and delightful though they are, the Buddhas may nevertheless frighten you. Do not give in to your fright! Do not run away! Serenely contemplate the spectacle before you! Realize that these are the rays of the grace of the Buddhas, who come to receive you into their Buddha-realms. Pray to them with intense faith and humility, and, in a halo of rainbow light, you will merge into the heart of the divine Father-Mother, and take your abode in one of the realms of the Buddhas. Thereby you may still at this moment win your salvation ...[12]

But lest his hearer should think he is now well informed about how things really are, in the next world, the lama continues 'It is from your own mind ... that all this has sprung. What you see here is but the reflection of the contents of your own mind in the mirror of the Void.'[13] In Tibetan Buddhism then, paradoxically, to find what one expects in the life to come is not to have one's religion verified, but rather to continue to be blinded by illusion.

Survival of human death, then, need not by any means result in the kind of unambiguous, solidly evidential situation Hick has in mind. The belief that 'then we shall know all', while it may be held on some religious ground, has little to support it otherwise, especially if any account is taken of the possible mediumistic evidence to the contrary. Some kind of public and unmistakable manifestation of God seems as much needed, in a life to come, as in the present life, if religious beliefs are to be

[12] Conze, ed., *Buddhist Scriptures*, p. 228.
[13] *Ibid.*, p. 229.

verified beyond question, in one decisive experience. 'Blessed are the pure in heart, for they shall see God', taught by Jesus in the Sermon on the Mount, has been in Christian theology the basis for a doctrine that, in the resurrected life, man may indeed be given some direct vision of the reality of God. Without some such lasting and collective face-to-face experience (whatever that might mean in the circumstances!) the conclusiveness of eschatological verification seems still in question.

LIMITS TO KNOWLEDGE IN A LIFE TO COME

One further criticism, which aims to show a basic weakness in the idea of verification in a life to come, is made by W. T. Blackstone in his book *The Problem of Religious Knowledge*. Religious language has its greatest problems when it tries to speak about God's unique, unlimited qualities—his omnipotence, omnipresence, perfect goodness, infinite love, etc. It is here that paradox and obscurity become most troublesome. Blackstone says:

> Even post-mortem experience, if there be such, could not be experience of God's unlimited, infinite characteristics. Finite beings cannot have experience of infinite characteristics. Therefore, even if we do have post-mortem experiences, we will still be confronted with the same epistemological problems concerning meaningful talk about God.[14]

Hick answers this objection, however, in the following way. He suggests that so long as post-mortem experience were sufficient to confirm the authority of someone like Jesus to act as spokesman for God, it would make it possible to take his word for the claims about God which cannot, by their very nature, be grasped through human observation.

> Our beliefs about God's infinite being are not capable of observational verification, being beyond the scope of human experience, but they are susceptible of indirect verification by the removal of rational doubt concerning the authority of Christ. An experience of the reign of the Son in the Kingdom of the Father would confirm that authority, and therewith,

[14] *The Problem of Religious Knowledge* (Prentice-Hall 1963), p. 122.

indirectly, the validity of Jesus' teaching concerning the character of God in his infinite transcendent nature.[15]

Once again, it might be necessary to give an account in non-religious terms of what kind of situation would reasonably support the taking of Jesus' words as an authority about God's unobservable characteristics. While that may be very difficult to spell out in the present life, there is no reason to suppose that some such situation could in principle not arise, given the possibility of an appropriate 'life to come'. As we shall see in the next chapter, taking someone's word for things we cannot ourselves test is a familiar, and often thoroughly reasonable, thing to do.

[15] Hick, *op. cit.*, p. 69.

6

TAKING SOMEONE'S WORD FOR IT

How do you know there is anything in the things you say about God? In the past few chapters we have looked at some kinds of testing and observation which might be used in trying to answer that question. But most practising Christians (or Jews or Muslims) would think the approach we have taken quite strange. 'Why be so tentative, so hesitant? . . .' they would ask. 'When *we* speak about God we speak confidently. We do not have to weigh every word, or wonder if we have grounds for each statement. For our religious language comes not from our own investigations, but from what we have been taught. We have it on good authority.'

There can be no doubt that when we look at the practice of religious believers, appeal to authority is quite central. Religious systems look back to their founders, and to others with specially important experiences. And they look to those prophets, witnesses, teachers, scholars and councils who have expressed in words the beliefs and interpretations by which they understand the foundation events of their faith, and their continuing experience of it. Believers in later times, then, know what to say and what not to, because they have learnt from those they take as their authorities. This enables them to speak confidently, to make claims and assent to things which go far beyond their own first-hand ability to check and test.

How, indeed, do we know how to talk about anything beyond our own immediate experience? Chiefly because we have learnt from others and go on learning. Discussing current affairs, planning a world tour, chatting about fashion—all this is learned behaviour. And a good deal of the learning process is copying what is done by someone we rely on, until we know enough to go on and make some fresh moves of our own. We will look more closely at the process of 'learning the religious language-game' in the next two chapters. Here it is enough to note how important the element of reliance on an authority is in explaining how it comes about that religious believers use the language they do. Ian Crombie has put it (from a Christian point of view) like this:

> The things we say about God are said on the authority of the words and acts of Christ, who spoke in human language, using parable; and so we too speak of God in parable—authoritative parable, authorized parable; knowing that the truth is not literally that which our parables represent, knowing therefore that now we see in a glass darkly, but trusting, because we trust the source of the parables, that in believing them and interpreting them in the light of each other, we shall not be misled, that we shall have such knowledge as we need to possess for the foundation of the religious life.[1]

(Notice that Crombie is speaking not only of the well-known Gospel parables told by Jesus, but of all that Jesus says about God, using what we have called *oblique* language.)

So long as you have an authority to rely on, then, you can use oblique, figurative language, believe in its informativeness and have your attitudes shaped and expectations aroused by it, even though you may not be able to give an account of what *makes* the language informative. Trusting an expert, in other words, is a valid alternative to making the necessary tests, in our search for reliable information. We are entitled to be reassured, when a reliable economist tells us 'the economy is healthier', though we ourselves don't know what makes his figurative remark factual. So, too, the speaker of religious language may rely on it far beyond his own ability to test it—because he draws on what he supposes to be the authority of experts in whom he trusts; people better placed than he, to know what they are talking about.

HOW CAN YOU TRUST IN WHAT YOU DON'T UNDERSTAND?

There are two objections philosophers bring to the idea of taking

---

[1] Antony Flew and Alasdair MacIntyre, ed., *New Essays in Philosophical Theology* (S.C.M. Press 1955), pp. 122-3.

the meaningfulness of oblique language 'on trust'. Kai Nielsen expresses the first, in a reply to Crombie.

This talk, tempting as it may seem to some, won't do.... Unless we understand what is meant by saying, outside of the parable and quite literally, that there is a God and he is merciful, how could we possibly trust that Jesus or any other religious authority is not misleading us in the parable, for we could not, if we did not understand the utterance literally in its non-parabolic context, know what could count as being misled or as failing to be misled by Jesus or by anyone else? Without some independent way of indicating what we are talking about when we are talking about God, we cannot understand what is meant by saying that the image or the parable *is or is not* faithful. And we cannot take on trust what we cannot understand, for we cannot know *what* it is we are supposed to take on trust.[2]

Bernard Williams makes the same point more briefly: 'If you do not know what it is you are believing on faith, how can you be sure that you are believing anything?'[3] This objection seems simply to deny that there can be a middle position between fully understanding, on the one hand, and having no idea at all, on the other. But the middle position is the usual one, in any learning situation. We have seen in chapter one the possibilities of increasing knowledge through the use of figures of speech. The very usefulness of oblique language lies in its suggestiveness. It raises a host of ideas, associations, connections, and so can be put to a range of possible exploratory uses which precise, literal language cannot. Oblique language may well be tentative, vague and easily misunderstood, yet can nonetheless be capable of pointing us in the right direction, and thus carrying genuine informativeness.

It is not impossible to take someone's word for something when we are unsure whether there are facts to fit the images their words arouse. We trust that the oblique impression the words evoke will turn out to be roughly right, at least, once

[2] 'On Fixing the Reference Range of "God" ', in *Religious Studies*, Vol. 2, No. 1, October 1966, pp. 13-36, at p. 29.
[3] 'Tertullian's Paradox', in Flew and MacIntyre eds, *New Essays in Philosophical Theology*, pp. 187-211, at p. 209.

we are in a position to make more precise tests. This is quite simply the usual way of learning to talk about some new not-directly-observable subject-matter. Think, for instance, of when we learnt about electricity, biology, or weather forecasting. Models, analogies, figures of many kinds were essential devices to give us our first understandings. We took such things on trust. In time we have come to know, perhaps, the observations which lie behind them and make them reliable analogies or apt models. But even before we did that, we possessed something of genuine factual content.

It does, then, make perfectly good sense to speak of taking on trust something conveyed to us by means of imagery or parable. We may not understand just what we are being asked to believe, but with some possible meanings in our minds, arising from the oblique terms themselves, we have sufficient to begin to take the subject seriously. To insist that 'faith cannot precede understanding' in the acquiring of new information, is to ignore the method by which we have all learnt a great deal of what we know.

HOW CAN WE CHOOSE AUTHORITIES
WITHOUT BEING AUTHORITIES OURSELVES?

The other philosophical objection to 'taking on trust' has to do with the idea of an *authority* itself. We may choose to treat someone y as an authority on something x. But if that choice is to be reasonable rather than capricious there must be grounds for thinking y to have special knowledge of x such that his words about x are worth relying on. But to know whether or not y *has* special knowledge of x, we presumably have to know something about x too. Yet how can we, if our only source of knowledge about x can be from an authority?

The paradox seems particularly severe in the case of religious knowledge, knowledge about God. Are there any experts in this field? If so, how can we know they are experts, without ourselves being able to judge whether they really do have the knowledge they appear to have? It is not so difficult where the authority is the person with expertise, the person who can do something well. The gardener, for example, who produces fine vegetables, wins prizes in flower shows, and can keep slugs away and avoid frost damage—he is seen to be an expert on gardening by what he can *do*. What he says will then be worth taking seriously.

Is there an analogy, in the case of knowledge about God? Some might say the expert on God and religion is the person who clearly is able to make sense of life, using religious categories of thought, and carrying out practices of worship and devotion. As H. H. Price says:

> Most of us nowadays have to begin by accepting the testimony of other seekers, who have already gone some way along the road and claim that it is leading them somewhere. Or rather, we begin not quite by accepting their testimony, but by taking it seriously because we are impressed by the kind of characters which they have.[4]

The chief problem, in judging religious experts, is the danger of an illusory impression of authority. We may be struck by a compelling personality, a long-standing institution, or a revered and ancient book. But if we rely simply on a sense of compulsion or impressiveness, that is something about which we may well come to change our minds. Remember how conclusive seems the first book we read on a new subject—until we come across others and find there is room for great differences of opinion. Think how authoritative anything can sound if expressed in a sufficiently striking form. It is not difficult to make up incantations and pronouncements which (like the Oracle at Delphi) gain impressiveness from being extremely general and apparently most profound, yet which to the non-suggestible hearer really say nothing much at all. The deliberate use of archaic, portentous-sounding language greatly increases this effect —a point not overlooked by latter-day prophets, spiritualistic mediums, or writers of tales about visitors from outer space (with their 'Hear ye, O dwellers on the planet earth ...' and the like).

Antony Flew warns us:

> Nor will it do to think that authority is something which can just be recognized as objectively there; and that is that.

[4] *Essays in the Philosophy of Religion* (The Clarendon Press 1972), p. 69.

Certainly one may learn to recognize the authoritative manner, the habit of command, the charismatic personality; and when we recognize them we may, or we may not, feel impelled to accept, to obey, to follow. Of course we know what it is to speak as one having authority. But no such seeming such can ever guarantee actually being an authority. In this case as in others appearances may be deceptive. To know that he, or it, is indeed a reliable authority you have to have some sufficient reason for believing that he, or it, knows what he, or it, is talking about.[5]

Some sort of rational checking of credentials, then, is called for wherever one's choice of an authority rests primarily on its impressiveness.

If some person, writing or organization claims 'The things we say are authoritative statements about God', it is proper to ask 'How could they possibly know?', and reasonable to hold back from accepting them as an authority until some satisfactory answer is given. That is not to suggest that there are no genuine religious authorities, or that it is never rational to trust any. There may well be, but if so their authoritativeness is not something to be taken as beyond question. While a believer may say 'I can't argue for it, I simply trust ...' (in such and such an authority) his trusting is not so simple as it sounds, for it rests on an assumption that the authority he trusts is able to carry the logical burden for his beliefs. That assumption may or may not be valid.

The establishing of authorities in religious matters is made still more difficult by the occurrence of what seem like (and often are) question-begging arguments. To illustrate this I shall look briefly at some features of the Christian view of the Bible as sacred, authoritative scripture.

THE BIBLE AS AUTHORITATIVE RELIGIOUS LANGUAGE[6]

The view most commonly held by Christians throughout their history, of their right to use religious language in the ways they

---

[5] *God and Philosophy* (Hutchinson 1966), p. 179.
[6] See also David Stacey, *Interpreting the Bible*, No. 4 in the 'Issues in Religious Studies' series. Sheldon Press.

do, has been quite simple. The Bible is the source of that authority. It contains not only the record of God's dealings with men and nations. It also gives the words in which God himself is to be talked about, his will for men known, and his way of salvation grasped. Though, on the face of it, the Bible consists of the writings of many different people, over more than ten centuries, yet they are all *inspired by God*, so that their words become his words. Being God's words the Bible is infallible. It may be misunderstood or misinterpreted, but it cannot in itself be in error.

A large number of active Christians today still hold that view of the Bible. At an International Congress on World Evangelism held in Lausanne during 1974, for instance, conservative evangelical Christians affirmed, among other things, 'the divine inspiration, truthfulness and authority of both Old and New Testament Scriptures in their entirety as the only written word of God, without error in all that it affirms, and the only infallible rule of faith and practice.'[7] What reasons do such Christians give for taking a diverse collection of sixty-six books, written by various Jewish and Christian authors, most of them unknown, as uniquely and exclusively the words of God? That view may have been the prevailing opinion of the Church until modern times. But can such a confident choice of a final verbal authority be given any rational basis today?

Defenders of the view argue that it is the Bible's own view of itself. It was the belief of the Jewish faith that God spoke through his prophets, and gave his teaching to men in the form of written *torah* or instruction. Phrases like 'God spoke to ...', 'Thus says the Lord ...', 'the word of the Lord ...', were applied not just to particular communications but, in time, to the whole corpus of sacred writings, forming a holy book, the Word of God. Similarly, in the New Testament, it is sufficient for a citation of an Old Testament passage to begin 'It is written ...' to claim it as having divine authority. Certain New Testament verses (notably 2 Tim. 3.16 and 2 Pet. 1.20–21) are taken to show explicitly the Bible 'witnessing to its own authority' as being of more than human origin, and the uniquely inspired and authoritative form in which divine revelation is given to man.

But of course 'the Bible's own view of itself' (even if a mean-

[7] Reported in *Time*, August 5, 1974.

ing for that phrase can be agreed upon) is still only binding on the Christian if he already believes the Bible to be authoritative in all its views. The argument in fact is circular—it assumes what it sets out to prove. Even if the Bible were totally authoritative, it could not be known to be simply because it appears to regard itself in that way. The sacred scriptures of many religions contain passages claiming for themselves unique divine authority. Unless one is prepared to say *all* such scriptures are what they claim to be, one must be ready to produce reasons external to the claims of the writings themselves for taking one as authoritative and not another.

The reason most commonly given nowadays in support of the traditional view of the Bible is that Jesus himself viewed his Bible (the Jewish scriptures) in that way. What better reason could there be, for those who take Jesus as the supreme revelation of God's will for mankind?

Certainly Jesus had a very high appreciation of the sacred books of his nation, finding in them much by which to express his understanding of God, and criticizing his contemporaries for their lack of knowledge of them (e.g., Mark 12.24). In the Gospel accounts he is shown as quoting from a wide range of Old Testament passages, taking them as prophecies of his own coming, ministry, death and resurrection. The Church has understandably seen this as an endorsement of the Jewish view of sacred scripture as inspired words from God, and applied the same reasoning to the writings that came to be included in the New Testament canon. But there is a good deal also to suggest that Jesus differed markedly in his use of the scriptures from the standard Jewish practice of his day. That he was not a strict literalist with regard to the Law is clear from his disagreement with the current official interpretations of its rules for Sabbath observance (Mark 2.27) and ritual washing (Mark 7.1–23). Nor must the allusions, in the course of his teaching and arguments, to the ancient stories of his people, necessarily be taken to imply that he took those stories as unquestionably factual historical narratives.

It is, of course, a greatly disputed question how much of the speech attributed to Jesus in the Gospels is in fact his own, and how much reflects the interpretative activity of the Early Church, concerned as they were to show that the events of Jesus's life

70

had indeed 'fulfilled the scriptures'. The subject is not one we can pursue here. What is important to notice for our purposes, however, is that whatever may be decided about the views and practice of Jesus with regard to scripture, it is a further question *why* the example of Jesus should be taken as decisive in this matter. To that question the Christians may well reply, 'Because he was the Son of God', 'Because he is our supreme revelation of God ... the Word made flesh', and so on. But to account for the authoritativeness of Jesus in those ways is again a question-begging procedure.

If Jesus is the supreme revelation of God, then his example in regard to the use of scripture will presumably be highly authoritative for the believer. But the belief that Jesus *is* the supreme revelation of God has itself to be defended. And if the main argument is that 'The Bible tells us so', the circularity becomes obvious: the authority of Jesus depends on believing the Bible to be authoritative about him; the authority of the Bible depends on accepting Jesus's view of the Bible. There is a way out of the circularity, but only at the expense of admitting that some reasons must be found for taking the Bible as authoritative, which go beyond arguments drawn from the Bible itself.

Many modern Christians find much about the Bible to discourage them from holding the traditional view that every word is to be taken as divine. Such a dogma, they feel, leads to unfortunate clashes with historical and scientific knowledge and the findings of literary studies of the scriptural writings themselves. It seems also to encourage uncritical assent to harsh moral and political views, vindictive pleasure in the downfall of unbelievers, and complacent acceptance of slavery, war, and racial and sexual inequality, simply because such things can be found 'in the Bible'. What case can be made for the Bible as an authority for Christianity without adopting the traditional 'infallible Word of God' view?

The traditional view discussed above may be called a *deductive* approach; it holds that because the words of the Bible are divinely inspired, truths about God can be simply deduced or read off from those words. In contrast to this is an inductive view, according to which divine inspiration is not uniformly presupposed, but the varying circumstances and intentions of the writings themselves are first of all taken into account. In general

71

terms, on this view, the Biblical writings represent many centuries of religious experience, and document the emergence and development of a living religious tradition. This gives the writings the authority of the work of specialists and significant contributors to a body of faith. In addition to that general authority, Christians find in the Bible a uniquely particular authority, insofar as they take it to be not just a record of developing religious insight, but an account of progressive acts of God, leading to an incarnation in the person of Jesus Christ, to achieve man's salvation and establish the beginnings of his Kingdom on earth. The New Testament picture of Jesus as the supreme 'specialist' on the subject of God becomes the standard by which all else, including the other biblical writings, is evaluated.

The inductive view has the advantage of treating the biblical writers as authorities independently of any taken-for-granted doctrine of the infallible authority of the whole Bible. The writings are to be taken seriously, on this view, because they are the records of those people and communities who had first-hand experience of unique happenings, were participants in the historical activity of God, experienced prophetic inspiration, were eye-witnesses to the person and ministry of Jesus and his resurrection appearances, and so on. What is more, many of them were themselves significantly changed by the religious experiences about which they write—so much so that they came to live like those who knew what life was about, who 'walked with God', and showed the quality of life which men came to describe as spiritual and eternal. This is, indeed, the very kind of authority several New Testament writers appear to claim for their writings (e.g., Luke 1.1–4; 1 John 1.1–4).

The Christian may want to go further, and believe that in the providence of God the testimony of those experts, those key witnesses and primary interpreters, has been recorded and preserved so that later generations too can share in the events from which the faith has sprung. The compiling and preserving of scriptures is itself to be seen as a gracious act of God. But the Bible's authority, on the inductive view, still lies not in its words as such, so much as in what it records and communicates to man today, of the progressive dealings of God with mankind, centred on his decisive self-revelation in Jesus Christ.

One main objection to an *inductive* view of the Bible by holders of the *deductive* position, is that the words of scripture are no longer seen as a supernaturally given, divinely authorized language in which men can truly speak about God. Scripture becomes merely the words of men, attempting to talk about God's non-verbal revealing of himself in events and experiences and history.

Much liberal Protestant theology in recent years has indeed discouraged the idea of *verbal* revelation. The chief reason for this has been a view of religious faith as a personal response to divine grace, rather than as assent to a set of truths stated in words. As the theologian John Baillie insists, '... in the last resort it is not information about God that is revealed but very God himself incarnate in Jesus Christ our Lord'.[8]

The suggestion that what is revealed is not truths about God but 'God himself', however, is rather misleading. If, as Christians hold, little can be known about God other than what he chooses to reveal, then in revealing true information in words about himself he would *be* revealing himself. Certainly there is a difference between faith as assent to propositions stated in words, and faith as a personal response to a gracious approach. But even to suspect that there is such a thing as a gracious personal approach on God's part is to have in mind certain supposedly factual propositions. For without assuming the truth of such propositions, why make one kind of response rather than another—or any response at all? To believe certain statements to be true of God then (e.g., that he is good, that he will save those who trust in him, that he has a plan for the universe, etc. ...) is not to substitute belief in sets of words for trust in a divine person. It is to trust in God as he is stated to be in those words and propositions. That trust may be as interpersonal as the believer finds he can interpret it—but it still presupposes a set of beliefs expressible in words and statements. There is clearly an important point for the Christian faith in the emphasis on God's revelation as being a personal self-manifestation rather

[8] *The Idea of Revelation in Recent Thought* (Oxford University Press 1956), p. 28.

than a set of authorized statements. Yet an otherwise unknown divine person might very well communicate not merely through historical events and mystical encounters, but as well through conveying suitable words and concepts for making sense of such phenomena. If it is believed that God can weave his revelatory acts into the texture of nature and history, there seems no reason at all to rule out the bringing about of human word-use in certain ways, as a crucial part of that revelation. This is indeed what conservative views of the Bible have been anxious to insist upon. B. B. Warfield, a classic exponent of Biblical inspiration and authority, says:

> No doubt, on adequate occasion, the very stones might cry out by the power of God, and dumb beasts speak, and mysterious voices sound forth from the void; and there have not been lacking instances in which men have been compelled by the same power to speak what they would not, and in languages whose very sounds were strange to their ears. But ordinarily when God the Lord would speak to men he avails himself of the services of a human tongue with which to speak, and he employs this tongue according to the particular nature of the tongue which he employs.[9]

However, to attempt to preserve the possibility of verbal revelation by insisting on a doctrine of total inspiration and infallibility for the words of the Bible, seems unnecessarily heavy-handed. If God is a supreme divine agent, anxious to communicate with man, he may very well do so through inspiring men to speak appropriate words at various times; formulating certain moral insights, making prophetic criticisms of current ideas, authorizing various myths and stories, concepts and ways of speaking, by which to grasp better the nature of God and his will for humanity. Allowing all that, however, does not oblige Christians to hold that the Scriptures as compiled by the Jewish nation and the Christian Church fully and for all time mark out the scope of God's revelation, either of his works *or* his words. To argue for the possibility of verbal revelation (authorized words about God, given by God) is one thing; to insist that every verse in the Bible, and nothing anywhere else, is to count as God's words, is quite another.

[9] *Biblical Foundations* (Tyndale Press edition 1958), p. 33f.

If, then, as an inductive view of scripture requires, the God-given words and concepts cannot be simply read off, but must be discerned and sifted out from amongst the historically conditioned human writings which mediate them, who is capable of the task of finding what words really are the authoritative ones? The Christian answer is that it is the function of the Holy Spirit to make these things clear, primarily within the shared thinking of the Christian community. This view may make certainty very difficult to obtain. But it need not necessarily lead to total subjectivism, and the subjection of scripture to human reason which defenders of the deductive view of the Bible quite understandably fear.

Human judgement, opinion and consensus can enter in without its following that what can be learned from scripture will be limited to human ideas about God. Suppose I receive what seems to be a message from an important Government official, giving me information and instructions highly relevant to my future well-being. And suppose the message is brought to me by word of mouth, by a rather puzzling intermediary from a different culture, speaking a foreign language, and by no means as well-informed about current affairs as I am. The fact that I think it proper to make some checks on whether the message is what it seems, whether the intermediary is likely to have got it right, and so on, does not mean that I am pitting my reason against the authority of the Government official. Nor does it follow that I can never have good grounds for taking from the message any information which I could not equally well have thought up for myself.

REVELATIONS ARE NOT SELF-EVIDENT

The possibility that religions are right in their belief in a communication of authorized words and images on God's part should perhaps make philosophers less ready to accept, uncritically, purely naturalistic explanations of the origins and nature of religious language. But admitting the possibility that God may actively reveal propositions and ideas about himself is quite a different thing from agreeing that believers are fully justified in their use of words, simply by their appealing, without further argument, to the notion of some authorized revelation.

The authority of sacred books or scriptures is not self-evident, even if that authority is taught by certain religious figures, themselves taken as authorities. Like any other appeal to authority, it needs to be backed up with reasons. No one can object to another's decision to treat a certain book, or religious figure, as authoritative about God, even when he cannot spell out grounds which make it reasonable to decide in that way. All that is necessary (to avoid arbitrariness and irrationality) is that he *believes there to be* such grounds. But that is a belief which may or may not be well founded.

As R. W. Hepburn says, considering the position of the Christian converted by the impact of Jesus upon him into accepting his authority as absolute:

> To appeal in this way to an unanalysable personal impact may, as I suspect, be a logically invulnerable procedure. It is not of course beyond another sort of challenge—from quite a different source. Just as different biographies, or paintings, of the same man may present violently contrasting impressions of their subject, so two readers of the New Testament may come away from their study of Jesus with two strongly contrasting pictures of his person, and with varying estimates of his authority. Discussion of the theological position that we have been examining would take the form ... of the comparison of and judgement between rival imaginative responses to the total New Testament witness to Jesus. Are we bowing the knee where it ought *not* to be bowed? Is our picture of Jesus dependent, as it should be, on the New Testament alone, or is it borrowing from sentimental literary and pictorial embroiderings? Are we being selective in the words and incidents in the Gospels that we allow ourselves to linger over; do we hurry over hard sayings and situations where in fact Jesus does not honestly impress us at all, but only puzzles us or bewilders us? [10]

What that amounts to is this: the Christian who justifies his words about God by an appeal to the language of Jesus which he takes as authoritative is not being illogical in doing so. But neither is his position self-evidently secure. There have been

---

[10] *Christianity and Paradox* (Watts 1958), p. 189f.

many others, informed and sensitive theists amongst them, who do not respond in the Christian way to the records of the person of Jesus or experience any authoritative impact from the New Testament; any more than most Christians respond to the records of the prophet Muhammad, or experience the impressiveness which the Muslim finds in the Qur'an.

'Taking someone's word for it', in religious matters, would make a great deal of sense if we knew for sure that the words in question were from God, or from some reliable authority. But the establishing of that position itself seems to depend on appeals to claims about divine sonship, inspired scripture, revelation, God speaking to men, and the like—the very kinds of religious statement we have seen to be most problematic.

By whatever means their authority is defended, the sacred scriptures of religions and the words of authoritative figures recorded in them must be recognized as fundamental in understanding religious language-use. They are the primary source of the stories, imagery, concepts and propositions used to express beliefs about God and the human condition. They provide the greatest fund of ideas for interpreting the continuing religious experience of believers and their communities. But the observation that religious people for the most part take their language on trust from the founders of their religions and the sacred scriptures of their traditions does not relieve the philosopher of his task of assessing the validity of that language. While it may show him the right place to begin his investigations, it in no way bypasses the questions about informativeness and testability which we have been considering in previous chapters.

7

DOING THINGS WITH
RELIGIOUS LANGUAGE

Most of the discussion so far has been about what I have called
religious claims or assertions. These are sentences which seem
to be stating that such-and-such is the case: 'There is no God
but Allah'; 'In the beginning God created the heavens and the
earth'; 'As in this body the embodied soul passes through child-
hood, youth and old age, in the same manner it goes from one
body to another'; 'Jesus Christ will return to judge the living
and the dead'. The reason for spending so much time on these
has been that they seem crucial to religious belief, and yet are
full of problems, from a philosophical point of view. But perhaps in narrowing attention to religious claims, without looking
more carefully at the contexts in which those claims are set,
the philosopher risks missing part of the point of what he is
investigating. In this chapter, therefore, I shall consider some of
the important things done with religious language besides using
it in making (or appearing to make) factual, informative claims.

If we put ourselves in a situation where religious language
is being genuinely *used* (and not just talked about, as we have
been doing); if we visit a church or synagogue service, for
instance, watch the consecration of a cathedral, go on a pilgrimage to Mecca, or join in a Hindu funeral, we will find that by far
the greatest part of the language used is for quite different
purposes from communicating information or asserting religious
truths. We have already, in chapter one, noticed the *affective*
side of religious language, its power to arouse, evoke, and change
emotions and attitudes. We must now notice that it is also
effective—it achieves things, it enables believers to live out their
beliefs, and to *do* various things, as part of their religious life.

It is useful to use the term *religious behaviour* to refer, in
general, to the ways (private and public, individual and collec-

tive) in which religious believers express their commitment to the central figures and truths of their tradition, and follow after the goals it offers them. Religious behaviour includes not only particular acts of worship or ritual, but also the whole surrounding web of habits, customs, attitudes and lifestyle characteristic of those who follow a particular faith.

The use of language within religious behaviour is generally *not* of the argumentative, fact-claiming kind. For in behaving, acting and responding one is taking one's religious beliefs for granted; accepting them, not defending them or wondering about them. We do not expect a tribesman, praying to his ancestors on some ritual occasion, to give us his reasons for belief in an after-life. We would not attend a church's prayer meeting hoping to hear a defence of the proposition 'God exists', or read Zen riddles looking for an argument that *satori* is not an illusion.

There are, when we come to look more closely than usual, a great many things to be done with language besides stating beliefs or arguing about facts. We ask questions, make requests, express feelings, reassure, inspire, seduce, denounce, pledge allegiance ... and so on. Utterances containing words and phrases may look very similar when not seen in use. But they do not all turn out to do anything like the same things. As Wittgenstein pictures it:

> It is like looking into the cabin of a locomotive. We see handles all looking more or less alike. (Naturally, since they are all supposed to be handled.) But one is the handle of a crank which can be moved continuously (it regulates the opening of a valve); another is the handle of a switch, which has only two effective positions, it is either off or on; a third is the handle of a brake-lever, the harder one pulls on it, the harder it brakes; a fourth, the handle of a pump; it has an effect only so long as it is moved to and fro.[1]

By looking at many other uses of religious language besides the (as we have seen) rather troublesome fact-stating ones, we can perhaps better appreciate their relative importance for religious behaviour as a whole.

We look first at a kind of word-use which philosophers have

[1] *Philosophical Investigations*, translated by G. E. M. Anscombe, 2nd edn (Blackwell 1958), para. 12.

in recent times called *performative*. Certain words, it has been noticed, when used properly in appropriate contexts, are effective not so much because of what they say, as because they *do* something. Performative words are used, for instance, when we vote for a motion by saying 'Aye', bid in an auction by shouting 'Fifty pounds', or adjourn a meeting with the words 'The meeting is adjourned'. There are also many things we can actually do simply by saying that we are doing them. For example, by using the words 'I thank you', 'I warn you', 'I promise', 'I hereby give devise and bequeath ...', 'We the undersigned protest ...', we can (if the circumstances are suitable) thank, warn, promise, dispose of our estate, protest, and so on. The words we use perform for us—they do things, or get things done, things which count as our actions, and for which we take the credit or blame. By using words, then, a good deal of the time we are doing things: entering into commitments, making and dissolving human relations, obliging ourselves to behave in various ways, and carrying out or breaking those obligations. A large part of our language-use, in other words, is for acting and involving ourselves, rather than for the mere passing on of information or asserting of beliefs.

Appreciating the performative functions of words can help throw light on what goes on in much of the use of language for religious purposes. The following examples will illustrate this.

WORSHIPPING

Some important acts of worship take place with very few words; their power lies not in what is said, so much as in some symbolic action or happening: the candles gradually being put out on the altar in the Orthodox Good Friday liturgy; the sharing of traditional foods in the Jewish Seder meal; the Buddhist's fixing of gold leaf to a pagoda; the actions of anointing, washing, marking with a sign, kneeling or prostrating oneself, and countless others found in all religions in one form or another.

Yet even for most of these, words are essential at some point, since it is words which provide the description under which such things *count as* acts of worship, and not just movements or happenings. It is because the religious description 'venerating the Blessed Sacrament' applies to it, that looking towards a wafer of unleavened bread in a box at the front of the church becomes a deeply meaningful thing for the devout Catholic to do. Similarly, it is because the words 'travelling to the world of spirits' fit the occasion, that the shaman's prancing on a hobby-horse becomes a serious business for the believers looking on. As we see in the case of worshipful silence, a surrounding describable in words sets the act in the appropriate light, making it profound and religiously pointful.

We must not think, of course, that a mere addition of words automatically converts the gesture or activity into something of religious importance. There are indeed religious practices in which words have a power of their own—even without being uttered or used (the mantras and prayers on Tibetan prayer-flags and prayer-wheels, for instance; or the use of words from the Qur'an, painted on a vehicle as a talisman). But in most cases it is the intentions, attitudes, and concentration of attention which accompany the performance, that make it fully an occasion of worship. The words help specify what *are* the relevant intentions and the appropriate attitudes. What is said brings out the meaning of what is done, and ties it to the behaviour and beliefs of the persons involved.

Obviously, too, there are times when words mark a turning-point within some larger, non-verbal activity. These are, in legal language, *operative* words. In the sacrament of Baptism, for instance, we find a striking example of the performative role of words. The utterance 'I baptize you in the name of the Father, the Son and the Holy Ghost', accompanied by the symbolic pouring, sprinkling or immersion in water, turns the happening into an effective Christian baptism. The same is true of other sacraments and ceremonies, where prescribed words used at certain key points are intended to make the whole activity achieve what it sets out to achieve.

But as well as words which play a supplementary, though sometimes a key part, within worshipful activities, there are also many occasions when words themselves form the chief means of worship. Then worship becomes, for the most part, a set of transactions carried on by speaking. Ninian Smart considers the language of worship in the following passage:

First, consider those utterances in worship which do not *say*

81

anything: such as the chant 'Holy, holy, holy, Lord God of Sabaoth'. To say 'Holy' is not to describe anything (though if it is uttered with sincerity the utterer will also doubtless believe that 'God is holy' states some kind of truth). It is, however, ascribing holiness to the Focus, and thus is properly used in addressing him ...

Why then do hymns and prayers so often go on to say things about God? Things, moreover, which are usually very well known to the hearers and presumably also to the Lord. The reason lies in the performative character even of these descriptions; for their function is celebratory. In telling God at Easter that he has raised his Son up from the dead, the worshipper is not reminding God or the congregation, but re-presenting the event. Thus as a general observation it is roughly true to say that stating descriptions is not a primary aspect of any worship.[2]

Ascribing qualities (like holiness) to God, and re-presenting past events, then, are two common kinds of language-use, both of which make it possible for believers to do things of a worshipful nature.

REMINISCING

Because words are able to bring to mind events, we can by means of them almost relive the experiences of the past, whenever we choose to do so. Children love to hear over and over some familiar story. They know they will not learn anything new at each fresh hearing. But they know too that enjoyable images, exciting sensations, will again be aroused in them. Adults, too, like to reminisce about 'the good old days', 'when times were hard', or about the exploits of their youth.

A large proportion of the narratives and stories told in religious contexts are of the reminiscing kind. 'Tell me the old, old story, of Jesus and His love', says the children's hymn. And the scriptures of ancient Israel stress the same theme, warning believers about the dangers of forgetting what kind of nation they are and what the Lord has taught them. 'Take heed ...

[2] *The Concept of Worship* (Macmillan 1972), p. 27.

lest you forget the things which your eyes have seen, and lest they depart from your heart all the days of your life;' (Deut. 4.9). Worship also includes reminders about the present. Christians proclaim 'Christ is risen' at Easter, and respond 'He is risen indeed'—not as a piece of fresh news, but as a truth to be remembered and allowed to colour their thinking and living here and now. And of course we can reminisce about the future— odd though it sounds to put it that way. Religious literature contains many forward-looking stories, which the faithful tell one another, again and again, to keep their hopes alive. (For some biblical examples see Isa. 35, 60; Rev. 21–22.)

Letting oneself be reminded of forgotten or half-forgotten things, hopes, or promises, plays a large part in Christian piety. It can be seen, for instance, in the systematic reading and re-reading of the Bible, the hanging of framed texts on walls, and regular attendance at church to sing familiar hymns and hear quite predictable sermons. One quaint form of reminder, probably little used nowadays, is the so-called promise-box, a boxed collection of suitable scriptural verses, each on a rolled slip of paper, from which one is taken at random from time to time, to encourage or challenge the believer. (A similar device has been used amongst Muslims for finding God's will for some special occasion.) The use of prayer-beads or a rosary, similarly, is found in several religions, as an aid to remembering one's prayers. Helping oneself to keep certain things in mind, then, is a quite fundamental part of religious devotional practice, and a great deal of religious language must be seen as serving this purpose.

COMMITTING

An important form of performative language is that by which we commit ourselves to certain things. We use words, as we have seen, to promise, make contracts, pledge loyalty and accept blame. We need only to think of the place of creeds, statements of faith, religious vows, dedications, confessions, and words of consecration within worship, to see how self-involving, commissive language makes it possible for believers to enter into obligations, or make deals with, their gods.

In the religion of Israel, the ancient Middle-Eastern covenant form for binding a lesser king to his imperial overlord became a model for the manner in which the nation Israel was bound to its Divine King, Yahweh. By formal words and ceremonies, the covenant was accepted and ratified. Each party became bound to the other. Embodied in the document were stipulations governing the dealings between the parties ('the Ten Commandments'), and lists of the benefits and sanctions (blessings and cursings) flowing from the keeping, or breaking, of the agreement. Thus by words and symbolic actions, believers bind themselves to God—and believe that he, too, binds himself to them in return through entering into the conventions of human language, with words providing the medium for divine-human interaction.

SOLEMNIZING

Many uses of religious words have the effect of solemnizing some natural occasion or occurrence, by setting it in a religious light. For example:

I name this ship *Cockleshell*, and may God bless her and all who sail in her.

This stone was laid to the Glory of God on 1 January 1890.

An offering for the Lord's work will now be received.

Certain verbal formulae are especially common for solemnizing purposes. The Muslim's *Bismillah* ('in the name of God') accompanies quite ordinary actions, like rising from sleep, putting on clothes, starting a journey or slaughtering an animal for food. Similarly the Christian formula 'In the name of the Father, and of the Son and of the Holy Ghost', plays many roles. So does the exclamation 'Thanks be to God!', by which some success or piece of good luck is received as an instance of divine providence.

INVOKING, PRAYING, BLESSING

Asking questions or making requests are further non-stating uses of words, as also are optative or 'wishful' expressions like 'if only ...', 'may it be so ...', or 'we pray that ...'. Many psalms and hymns are in the form of prayers, either asking, or expressing a desire or wish which is believed to be in accord with the will of God and so proper to express in his hearing. Benedictions (the asking of blessings on something or someone) are a special case of invocatory prayer. In many blessing phrases (like 'God be with you', 'the Lord bless you', 'Peace be unto you') a combination of request and performative utterance is involved. By asking God to protect, give peace, etc., one is oneself giving something to another. One's utterances of blessing or well-wishing (like cursing or ill-wishing) can then be seen almost as negotiable instruments, like cheques drawn on God. The swearing of oaths, again, is a way of solemnizing one's words by invoking God as a witness or guarantor of what one says, vows or promises.

EXHORTING

More words are used publicly in religion for *exhorting* than for any other purpose. This commonly takes the form of urging or encouraging others to join in worshipful activities: singing praises, praying, making gifts and sacrifices, humbling oneself and so on. Stirring up worshipful behaviour in others comes to be itself a sort of worship. It is like the task of the cheerleader, who helps his team by directing his efforts towards rousing supporters and calling on them to be more wholehearted in their cheering. Well-known phrases from the Psalms all have that indirect approach. 'Praise the Lord', 'Give unto the Lord glory and honour', 'Sing to the Lord a new song', 'Make a joyful noise ... serve the Lord ... come before his presence ...' They appeal to men to worship God in various ways, and thus become acts of worship themselves. Exhorting may also be directed to non-believers, as a challenge inviting a religious response. 'Choose you this day whom you will serve!' 'Come forward for Christ.' 'Repent, and believe the Gospel!' Warnings, too, are a way of impressing on non-believers the risks they are taking in their unbelief.

A different kind of exhorting is found, very commonly in Christian preaching, in the New Testament epistles, and in devotional writing (Thomas à Kempis's *The Imitation of*

Christ is a classic example, with countless similar works, ancient and contemporary). It takes the form of exhorting to obedience, right conduct, spirituality and maturity of faith. This is a 'bread and butter line' in religious language-use. Take it away, and the shelves of religious bookshops would be largely bare, and many sermons and homilies reduced to a few sentences.

Urging on to a richer spiritual life may be done in many ways. The following examples from St Paul's Letter to Romans show some of the best-known forms: emphatic words of challenge ('I appeal to you therefore, brethren, by the mercies of God, to present your bodies as a living sacrifice, holy and acceptable to God'); examples from the lives of others ('Let each of us please his neighbour for his good, to edify him, for Christ did not please himself'); conclusions drawn from agreed premises ('If God is for us, who is against us?'); personal witness ('I am not ashamed of the gospel'); rhetorical questions ('How can we who died to sin still live in it?'); or simply lists of imperatives, hammering home the qualities of life expected of the believer ('Let love be genuine; hate what is evil, hold fast to what is good; love one another with brotherly affection; outdo one another in showing honour. Never flag in zeal, be aglow with the Spirit, serve the Lord. Rejoice in your hope, be patient in tribulation, be constant in prayer.').

It is impossible to do justice to the sacred scriptures of most religious traditions, or their public utterances, if we fail to notice just how much of the language is used, not to make claims about supernatural realities, but to urge on believers in their chosen ways of life. Open at random the Bible, the Qur'an, the *Bhagavad Gita*, the Talmud, *Sayings of Confucius* or *Teachings of the Buddha*, and you will seldom have to read for long before you find some kind of exhortatory language.

INSPIRING

Closely related to exhorting is the use of language in religion for inspiring, arousing feelings and stimulating actions. Like exhorting, inspiring is very much an *affective* function of words.

We have already noted the psychological power of religious stories and imagery to reinforce commitments to a certain way of life (see above, chapter three). Historical novels, religious drama (e.g., Passion plays), allegories (like C. S. Lewis's *Screwtape Letters* or Bunyan's *Pilgrim's Progress*), poetry and songs, rock-operas and oratorios, are but a few obvious examples of inspirational religious language-use. Lives of the saints, diaries of missionaries and pilgrims, accounts of conversions and changed lives, always popular amongst religious readers, similarly have an inspirational function.

Many writers on religious language, anxious to distinguish factual statements from non-factual, have given the impression that the *emotive* power of words in religion is largely unimportant, and more often than not rather disreputable. 'Appealing mostly to the emotions', and similar expressions commonly seem to suggest 'not up to much'. For that reason, the inspirational and affective force of the language used in religion seldom receives a positive treatment. But any who study the relations between beliefs and moral behaviour quickly realize how the emotional life of a person forms a very important background to his moral judgement and action. Emotions can be educated, matured, and harnessed in the service of good, and the part religious words play in this task is not one to be overlooked.

Most philosophers nowadays rule out any strict logical connection between morality and religious belief. But none would deny that where a person has religious emotions and attitudes, these may well play a very important part in shaping and motivating his morality. The function of religious language, then, in inspiring certain kinds of action, sensitizing feelings, reinforcing certain dispositions, and so on, is far from being a secondary or trivial matter. The popular idea that religion stirs up the emotions and makes them even more unmanageable than usual may be based on observing one side of religious behaviour —the more abandoned and ecstatic side. But there is another side, which the great religions have also all sought to promote: that of the discipline of the emotions, and their careful subjection to higher spiritual ideals. The Buddhist scholar Ashvaghosha wrote: 'The man who has imposed strict mindfulness on all he does, and remains as watchful as a gatekeeper at a city-gate, is safe from injury by the passions, just as a well-guarded town is safe from its foes.' The writer of Proverbs said much the same: 'A man without self-control is like a city broken into and left without walls.'

RELIGIONS AS LANGUAGE-GAMES

It must be clear by now that understanding religious language requires a thorough awareness of the kinds of situation in which it is learnt and used. It can only be fully appreciated by discovering the many parts it plays in an even wider environment, that of the behaviour and whole way of life followed by any group or society possessing a religious tradition.

Learning a religion and understanding the language it uses is rather like learning to play a game. That analogy has recently been used by some philosophers trying to give an adequate account of religious language-use. They have not suggested that religions *are* games. But there are many features of games which can help us grasp important things about language and its connections with religious belief and behaviour.

We rarely if ever learn a new game by first memorizing the rule book and then beginning to make the moves. We tend, rather, to pick up the rules while trying to play. So too, religious language is picked up, almost always, through participation, through following others who know more than we do about how to proceed. The main moves are learnt first, for the new convert will be anxious to find his place in the life and worship of the community of belief. The finer details come later, and he need not ever become an expert or theoretician, any more than most of us who play games are experts in the practice or theory of them.

Games are not, of course, played simply by following rules. The rules help define what kind of game they are, and what actions or events within them count as valid and invalid moves, scores, faults, penalties, etc. They also specify what counts as winning and what as losing. But there are a vast number of things the rules say nothing about, things which take place within the framework set out by the rules, but are not entirely dictated by them. These are things like set patterns of play, particular choices amongst possible moves, skills, tactics, training and practice, and the emotions that go with playing, like endurance, team-spirit, excitement and satisfaction. All this makes up the context of rules, behaviour, and emotional surroundings, within which each detail of the game has its final significance. We have seen that the same is true of the details of religious language and behaviour. It is easy enough to think up religious parallels to rule-books, team-spirit, physical fitness, learners and professionals, coaching and practice, wins and losses, and so on.

A further similarity is that there are, in most games, certain terms and concepts which only have a meaning because of their special part within the game. There is no such thing as a 'forward pass' taking place amongst rugby spectators or in the changing-rooms, for instance. The concept has an application only in the field of play. No player can be penalized for being 'off-side' after the game is over. Nor does it make proper sense to ask whether the referee, the groundsmen, or the timekeeper, were on the winning, or the losing side (though there are occasions when that question is asked sarcastically!).

In the case of religion, too, we have seen that some questions about religious ideas and activities do not make sense when they are asked outside the proper context in which they have their meanings. It is only when we are engaged in the Jewish and Christian religious language-games that the question 'Was Jesus the Messiah?' can be properly understood, and as we know, it is answered differently within each of those two language-games. Similarly there would seem little point in arguing about whether or not Hera really is the wife of Zeus, or Tane genuinely the son of Rangi and Papa, except when one is talking within the thought-worlds of classical Greek religion or Maori mythology. The same is true, equally, of the many actions, gestures and forms of worship which make up religious behaviour. They mean what they do because of their connections with other parts of the religious system and its thought-world.

Statements in religious language, like moves in games, are context-dependent. It has thus become quite common amongst philosophers of religion to speak of the way language is used in a certain religious tradition as the 'language-game' of that religion. That way of speaking is a useful reminder that misunderstanding and confusion are likely to result if statements are taken away from their context, and analysed without regard to the usual circumstances in which they are uttered, the moves they are used to make, and the point of the game as a whole. Whether the notion of religious 'language-games' is particularly helpful in other ways will be considered in the next chapter.

8

TREATING RELIGIONS AS LANGUAGE-GAMES

Just as games can only be properly understood when they are seen as something to be played, so religious language can only be properly understood when it is seen as part of a way of living. We found in the last chapter how the idea of a language-game has been used to throw light on the various uses of words found in religious systems. In this chapter I shall consider some of the less satisfactory consequences of taking the *game* model too seriously in a philosophical approach to religious language.

Religious tradition, language and behaviour have increasingly become subjects of interest to the social sciences, like sociology and anthropology. Their general approach to religions goes very roughly like this: there is always some point in any activity that continues to be carried on amongst human beings in their groups and societies. To appreciate the activity's point, one must be prepared to involve oneself in the social and intellectual life of the society where it is found. And then, what counts as reasonable or unreasonable, meaningful or absurd, will have to be decided by the standards of those who carry on the activity, and not by some external standards (like those of the anthropologist's own society).

Some recent writers about religious language, influenced especially by Wittgenstein's theory of language-games, have recommended a similar approach, from a philosophical point of view. For many people religious language does a unique sort of job, meeting certain of their needs, strengthening their family and social ties, giving them a way of expressing certain deep feelings, and so on. Since it works, the language-use is presumably in order as it is, once seen from the user's point of view, within his language-game and way of life. The fact that difficulties may be found in that language from other points of view is scarcely relevant. The criteria of the meaningfulness of religious concepts, and the standards by which words like *reasonable*, *meaningful* and *true* apply, 'are to be found within religion itself', D. Z. Phillips tells us.[1]

W. D. Hudson summarizes the argument thus:

> Religious belief can only be understood *from within*; and it is immune to charges of incoherence, unintelligibility, irrationality, or non-accordance with objective reality, *from without*, because, like any other universe of discourse, it sets its own definitive criteria of coherence, intelligibility, rationality and reality.[2]

Does this approach, sometimes called 'conceptual relativism' (because it argues that the meaning of concepts is completely relative to their context), relieve us, whether we are believers or sceptics, from the difficult questions about testing and justifying supposedly factual claims, which in previous chapters we have taken to be the chief problem of religious language? May we not simply accept that religious language is meaningful and valid for those who genuinely use it, and not worry whether there are any reasons, external to the religious way of life, by which it can be justified for those who do not participate in that language-game?

In some ways, what the conceptual relativists say sounds very like what many religious people have said. Do not believers commonly insist that you can't expect to understand unless you believe; that God's ways are hidden from those who approach with worldly wisdom, and revealed only to those who enter 'the circle of faith' in childlike trust? There is a strong tradition in Christianity (represented more extremely in Tertullian, Pascal and Kierkegaard, and more moderately in St Paul, Luther and Barth) which argues for such a 'fideistic' position.[3] And at a popular level we are often assured that 'for those who believe,

---

[1] *The Concept of Prayer* (Routledge & Kegan Paul 1965), p. 12.
[2] 'On Two Points against Wittgensteinian Fideism', *Philosophy* (1968), p. 269.
[3] For a discussion of the history of this position in Christian philosophy of religion see M. J. Charlesworth, *Philosophy of Religion: The Historic Approaches* (Macmillan 1972), chapter 3.

no argument is necessary; for those who do not believe, no argument is possible'.

But a little more thought shows that the consequence of a total conceptual relativism would be quite unacceptable to most believers, and would not really support the fideistic position at all. The problem is that despite what fideism seems to say (that we must rely on faith, not on knowledge) the very notions of having faith, trusting, believing, accepting and the like do not operate in an intellectual vacuum. They presuppose certain things—things which have traditionally been thought of as factual claims; for example, that there *is* someone to trust, some truth to accept, some state of affairs to hope for. In other words, there are things to be known, questions of fact, which even the most ardent fideist will want preserved and defended. It is all very well for him to say that Christianity is a language-game the meaning and truth of which can only be known to the players. But he is very likely, as a Christian, to want also to say that Christianity is true as against other possible language-games; that it is more reasonable than, say, witchcraft, truer to experience than Hinduism, and an advance, spiritually, on Judaism. Yet if conceptual relativism is accepted, no such comparisons can be made. If criteria of reasonableness, justification, factuality, apply only *within* one's system of belief, no one language-game has the possibility of deeper truth or superior knowledge than any others.

HOW CAN THE SCEPTIC DISAGREE WITH THE BELIEVER?

On the face of it nothing would seem more obvious than that a sceptic and a believer are in disagreement with one another. One says 'There is a God', the other says 'There is no God'. One claims 'The world is God's creation', the other denies that claim. But on the language-game theory, disagreements, claims and counterclaims, affirmations and denials, can take place only within language-games, for it is from the rules of the game (the conceptual system) in question that we understand what *counts as* agreement and disagreement.

A look at how religious and non-religious people talk to one another about religion, however, shows that religious language-use is by no means the 'Members Only' kind of activity which the language-game theory has been taken by some to imply. In a society where religious language-use can no longer uniformly be taken for granted, the non-user may have reasons for holding that he understands religion even better than the believer. He sees it for what it is, he may think, appreciating only too well its internal logic—and that is why he rejects it.[4] When faced with such a sceptic, the believer may try to insist 'but he doesn't really understand'. But that is hardly plausible, at least in the crucial case where the sceptic is someone who himself formerly did believe, i.e., who did play the language-game as an insider, but does so no longer. Here, the most obvious explanation of how the two parties differ is that the believer makes a favourable assessment of the things he takes as supporting his belief, while the unbeliever makes an unfavourable assessment, considering the evidence unconvincing and so rejecting the belief. This is not to say that the disagreement between believer and sceptic is a simple disagreement over a factual issue. It is much more complex than that; but the complexity arises from the obscurity of religious fact-claims and the tests relevant to them, not from the parties to the dispute operating with totally different concepts of fact, evidence, and reasonableness of belief.

It is, then, a misleading over-simplification to treat religious language as a self-contained system, entirely insulated from language used in other ways. Religious believers today are aware of more alternatives to systems of religious thought and language than ever before. If conceptual relativism were true, that state of affairs would have no particular bearing on the decline of religious belief and practice. But in fact, an increase in secular knowledge is the cause of many people's giving up religion. The religious language-game ceases, in their view, to have any longer the meaning they once found in it, because its fundamental assumptions as to the facts they no longer find credible.

Conceptual relativism, as Nielsen points out, fails to account for:

> people who play the language-game, even people who *want* very much to go on playing the language-game of religion,

---

[4] Cf. Alasdair MacIntyre, 'Is Understanding Religion Compatible with Believing?' in Hick, ed., *Faith and the Philosophers* (Macmillan 1966), pp. 115-33.

but [who] morally and intellectually speaking cannot continue this activity because their intellects ... make assent to Jewish or Christian doctrine impossible.[5]

Such people are not able to console themselves with the view that the religious language-game can still be played, by totally insulating it from the apparently conflicting issues raised in other areas of knowledge. Those on the other hand who do retain their religious beliefs while accumulating other knowledge commonly do so with increasing awareness of apparent inconsistencies which their religious claims raise in relation to the other things they know and say. This is an intellectual tension with which they live, continually looking for ways of reconciling religious and secular beliefs, and perhaps trusting, as a matter of faith, that such reconciliations exist and can be found if they look hard enough. To suggest that if they viewed their religious language correctly (as a closed system) they would not feel any such tension is quite implausible. They, the religious language-users, are the ones to say whether or not there is a tension between their religious claims and anything else they believe or know. And that is just what they do say.[6]

There are other features of religious language-use which also show it to be not entirely separate from the business of reason giving, fact claiming, and assertion making. Religious traditions always have their *apologists*, those who argue for the truths claimed in the system, trying to find common ground in reasoning between believers and non-believers. The attempt to offer reasons why people should believe is quite central in the practice not only of the universal religions but also, significantly, in more recent religious movements which seek to gain converts from amongst modern, secular-minded people. Thus apologists for the Baha'i World Faith appeal to the reasonableness of a syncretistic faith in today's pluralistic world. Christian Scientists claim to have, in spiritual healings, evidence to convince the open-minded questioner about the truth of their beliefs. The Transcendental Meditation movement makes wide use of the results of medical experiments as testimony to the benefits it has to offer. Jehovah's

[5] Kai Nielsen, 'Wittgenstein Fideism', in *Philosophy* (1967), p. 196.
[6] See, for instance, David Edwards' discussion of the impact of secularism in his *Religion and Change*. Hodder & Stoughton 1969,

Witnesses argue from the fulfilment of prophecy in contemporary events. Krishna Consciousness devotees offer mystical experience without the expense and dangers of drug-use. In all these cases, what is said on behalf of the religion goes beyond its own language-game and form of life, and seeks to attract others by appealing quite explicitly to beliefs, hopes or wants shared by non-believers.

Indeed, it could be argued that the main reason for the preaching of religious views beyond the confines of the community of religious language-users themselves has been not merely to make converts but to declare and proclaim *truths*. Religious systems have been believed not only to offer spiritual satisfaction and the meeting of various needs, but to contribute to an overall understanding of how things really are, for all men, believers and unbelievers alike. The language-game view of religions seems to represent the differences between believer and non-believer as simply a difference between those who do not make use of religious ways of talking, and those who do. While this may be how it appears, from the point of view of the non-believer, it is very odd to suggest that the believer will go along with that analysis. More normally we would expect him to hold very firmly that, sooner or later, the non-believer will find himself in a position where his present inability to see any point in religious claims and stories will be something he will have cause to regret.

> Every one who hears these words of mine and does not do them will be like a foolish man who built his house upon the sand.   Matt. 7.26–7

> The gates of heaven shall not be opened for those that have denied and scorned Our revelations; nor shall they enter the gardens of Paradise until a camel shall pass through the eye of a needle.   Qur'an, Surah 7 (The Heights)

> The fool, while sinning, thinks and hopes, 'This never will catch up with me'.
> But later on there's bitterness, when punishment must be endured.   Sanskrit *Dharmapada*

Whatever the imagery of such warnings is to be taken to mean in detail, it is hard to imagine their point being anything other than the assertion that there is an objective and fundamental difference between the believer and the non-believer, a difference as to the truth of their respective positions. Religions may be quite mistaken in making such (admittedly intolerant) claims. There may be nothing in them, and no justification for the warning they appear to give, about the dangers of unbelief. Yet despite the great diversity to be found amongst the religions of the world and the obscurity of the claims of even the most thought-over of them, it is simply a misrepresentation of religions to ignore their claims to tell us (in their oblique and puzzling ways) *what is so*, regardless of whether everybody, or even anybody, acknowledges it to be so, or finds any point in the language in which it is claimed to be so.[7]

LESSONS TO LEARN FROM THE LANGUAGE-GAME THEORY

In chapter seven we looked at many instances where utterances in religious language are used not to give information or state beliefs, but to express worship, to warn, promise, exhort, solemnize, and make possible a great many other pieces of individual and social behaviour. It became clear that one could not understand the words used in religious contexts unless one saw their links with these affective and behavioural features of a whole religious way of living. But the close relation that exists between religious behaviour, and the words used to express the related beliefs, is not so close that we may assume, because we have shown connections of language to behaviour and attitudes, that we have therefore shown *what the belief comes to*—as though there could not still be any further question about the intelligibility and truth of the beliefs, and the possible justifications for holding them, as beliefs with factual, informative content.

One serious defect of the language-game approach is that it has the effect of treating the meaning of religious utterances as nothing more than the role they have in the lives of the users, as members of a society or group in which that language-game is played. But asking 'What job does uttering such and such a form of words do for the utterers?', though no doubt a good starting

[7] For a thorough discussion of the limitations of conceptual relativism and the language-game view of religion, see Roger Trigg, *Reason and Commitment*. Cambridge University Press 1973.

point, may not exhaust the possible content of the words in question. They may have more to tell us—more, for instance, which may help explain why it is that *those* words, rather than others, have the effects they appear to have on the behaviour and attitudes of the users.

It is perhaps not irrelevant to notice how a great number of modern studies of religion have been based on investigations of the more bizarre sects and cults, or of so-called 'primitive' societies, where the sophisticated observer can scarcely avoid assuming that the claims to knowledge he finds in the language-use cannot possibly be taken at face value. This conclusion may be reached philosophically (for instance in the case of Braithwaite and Miles who, as we saw in chapter three, give philosophical reasons for discounting the possibility of talking about supernatural states of affairs). Or it can be reached simply by the argument that 'no one would utter such nonsense or believe such obvious absurdities unless it *did something* important for them'. So once we find what it does for them (what social or psychological functions it achieves, for instance), we have found what the apparent nonsense and the incredible beliefs *really* mean, and that is that.

In their increasing awareness of the inadequacy of that kind of approach, sociologists of religion are taking more seriously the importance of the supposedly cognitive, informational element in religion. The social anthropologist Clifford Geertz says:

> The tracing of the social and psychological role of religion is ... not so much a matter of finding correlations between specific ritual acts and specific social ties—though these correlations do, of course, exist and are very worth continued investigation, especially if we can contrive something novel to say about them. More, it is a matter of understanding how it is that men's notions, however implicit, of the 'really real' and the dispositions these notions induce in them, color their sense of the reasonable, the practical, the humane, and the moral.[8]

[8] 'Religion as a Cultural System', in Michael Banton, ed., *Anthropological Approaches to the Study of Religion* (Tavistock Publications 1966), p. 41.

Geertz is insistent that essential to religions is the attempt to say something about the meaning of things, to symbolize some features of reality not adequately grasped by the other meaning-systems with which man operates (e.g., commonsense, science, art).

The question, then, is whether in studying religions we are looking not only at the effects of men's beliefs upon their lives and societies, but also at the effects of that which is believed in. Any adequate approach must be prepared to take account of the possible actuality of the supposed objects of belief. Thus John Bowker argues after studying attempts to explain the human sense of God through the disciplines of sociology, anthropology and phenomenology:

> It no longer seems possible to assume, as it was usually assumed until very recently, that the claimed objects of belief are irrelevant to the analysis of believing behaviour. Far from the disciplines we have been surveying dissolving the possible reality of reference in the term 'God', they actually seem to demand a return to that possibility if sense is to be made of their own evidence.[9]

The strength of the language-game theory we have been considering is that it helps us to see how far-reaching are the consequences of belief for behaviour, and how subtle and various a part the language associated with the beliefs has to play in the working out of these consequences. But there remains the problem: does the language have not just a behavioural and affective function, but also an informative content, by which the behaviour itself, and the accompanying attitudes and emotions, can be evaluated as to their appropriateness? We return, in other words, to the nagging question raised in the Introduction: granted that religious language does all these things for people, are they being misled, or are they to some extent informed truly, and guided rightly by the words they utter and the claims they express?

The final chapter will suggest how the task of answering that question can be approached.

[9] *The Sense of God* (The Clarendon Press 1973), pp. 181-2.

9

FINDING MEANINGS AND GETTING
AT THE TRUTH

Religions are systems of belief and behaviour by which meanings are found in a very wide range of things encountered and
experienced in human life. The language of religious traditions
is the chief means by which people can interpret what they take
to be religiously meaningful phenomena. Not all interpreting is
in words. People may interpret by their reactions, rituals, and
other forms of behaviour with which they respond to and express
the meaning they find in things. But verbal interpretation is
generally more important than any other kind, especially in the
universal religions which depend very much on language for
expressing and transmitting themselves. It is through examining
the interpretative function of religious language that I shall
attempt, in this final chapter, to draw together the various topics
we have considered, and in particular to say something about
how questions of *truth* may be dealt with in the case of religions.

In very broad terms, what happens in religious interpreting
can be described thus: the kinds of things in life found in one
way or another to be religiously significant by those who practise
religions are taken to have meanings over and above their
scientific, historical or every-day meanings. These distinctively
religious meanings they attempt to grasp and communicate
through the use of words, concepts, imagery, or stories drawn
from the traditions of religious belief. The things they interpret
include historical events, dreams and inspirations, pangs of
conscience, mystical experiences, strange coincidences, victories
and defeats in battle, charismatic personalities and authoritative-
seeming writings and so on ... all the vast range of things we
call *religious phenomena.* The language used to interpret provides
a link between those things, and human reactions, commitments,
hopes and expectations, illumination and insight, despair, peni-

tence and worship ... the equally vast and varied collection of responses we call *religious behaviour*. The behaviour is a response to the supposed significance of the phenomena, interpreted by the language. The phenomena, by their past occurrence and to some extent continuing availability, make the behaviour seem appropriate and give the language points of contact with life, thereby making it plausible.

The accumulated language-use of religions, then, their sacred stories, theologies, devotional and liturgical works, their imagery, concepts and metaphysics all enable men to find meanings of a profound and sometimes all-important kind in features of the world, the past history of their race or civilization, and the particular events of life from day to day. Just as the person who has begun to study logic finds a new dimension of interest in the arguments used by people about him, or the geomorphologist while travelling takes special notice of the mountain scenery he views from his coach window, so the person who picks up some religious language and the attitudes and reactions that go with it has a way of finding new meaning and unexpected significance in things, through the activity of religious interpretation. Interpreting in religious terms is an indefinitely extendable process; new uses of certain key ideas and interpretations can be created, new applications generated, in much the same way as a child's construction kit permits us to put a set of basic components to endless new uses. Having mastered some rules of religious language-use, we can explore the world and our experience in new ways. Naturally if a maker of religious interpretations is also a member of a group or institution committed to holding a certain standard set of interpretations, some checks will be placed on the 'constructions' he comes up with. But while most religious groups do function so as to preserve certain norms and dogmas, it is not necessary that they must. There is nothing to stop anyone making up his own religion, and indeed many people do, using interpretative language from a variety of sources, and not feeling particularly bound by any existing orthodoxies.

FROM INTERPRETATIONS TO TRUTH-CLAIMS

I have spoken of how the religious person learns some interpretative ways of talking as he comes to participate in a religious way of life. What we must now notice is that, in associating himself with a religious system, he also learns a set of phenomena which are considered to make the interpretations in that system reasonable or plausible. Among these are certain past happenings, the classic foundation events of a religion (whether historical or legendary) the standard interpretations of which make the religious tradition what it is. But the phenomena include also recent or contemporary and even quite everyday phenomena available to the believer and the community of believers. These too are open to being interpreted in the light of those foundation events and their interpretations. A person's day by day questions about what he ought to do, what is really important in life, how secure is his future, whether there are spiritual resources he can turn to, and the like, are met with answers, explanations, and encouragements, insofar as he finds he can adopt for himself the interpretations of things which religious ways of speaking offer. Puzzlement and awe at the grandeur of nature can be expressed with the help of the poetry of the Psalms or the Genesis creation stories; feelings of responsibility for one's family and fellow-men can be understood in the light of the parables by which Jesus interpreted such things; a sense of forgiveness from guilt, after repentance and worship, can be appreciated with the help of talk about reconciliation with God and justification by faith, and so on. In such cases a present-day finding-of-religious-meaning draws on the language and images of a religious tradition, applying them to things here-and-now which count as what may be called *feedback*, showing that the interpretative system still works or fits. The activity of interpreting (through the use of religious language) thus links the beliefs and claims of a religion with past and continuing phenomena which are thought to manifest the reality of the objects of those beliefs, and thus to show the truth of those claims. Some of those phenomena will be extraordinary and perhaps unique, others quite ordinary and familiar.

But are we then forced to conclude that, since religious beliefs rest on interpretations, there cannot be any question of their objectivity or truth? Convinced believers naturally resist a word like *interpretation*, which seems to lead down a slippery slope into subjectivity and relativism, making religious beliefs simply a matter of private opinion. Surely if they are to be objectively true, religious claims must be *descriptive* and not just interpretative.

The difference between calling something a description and calling it an interpretation may, however, reflect little more than a difference in point of view. A claim which to the person who makes it seems certain and unquestionable, he will naturally hold to be a description. To an observer, however, not so convinced that the facts support what is claimed, it will seem rather to be an interpretation or opinion. But admitting that religious claims are more in the realm of opinion and interpretation than in the realm of definite description need not involve giving up the ideal of objectivity and truth. For as we know well enough, opinions may be good ones, interpretations may be correct, models may be accurate, and if they are, the statements expressing them can certainly count as true statements.

If interpretations can lead to truths, then, in what circumstances *do* they? We may recall a point from the first chapter, about the evocative and affective use of oblique language. We noted that its power to arouse emotions and bring to mind ideas was not a good guide to its informative content. The same is true of interpretations. The apparent impressiveness with which certain ways of speaking can seem to bring out profound meaning and deep significance in things is no guarantee that there is really anything like that meaning there. Over-interpreting is a constant danger, in any situation where we are trying to express the meaning of something ambiguous, suggestive but not clear. There is a vast difference between reading meaning into something, and actually discovering that meaning there. This possibility, of misinterpretation and especially over-interpretation, lies behind the sceptic's question: 'How can we be sure that religious believers, in their apparent discovery of profound meaningfulness, are not simply playing an elaborate game of make-believe?'

GETTING AT THE TRUTH IN RELIGIONS

It may seem quite natural to ask of religions 'Are their claims in fact true?', 'Do their beliefs correspond to reality?' But questions about truth are not always as simple as those words suggest. Truth in certain obvious and everyday situations can be simply a matter of correspondence between descriptions and observable-by-the-senses states of affairs. But even in many ordinary cases it is not like that at all. There are other ways of telling the truth besides describing perceptible states of affairs; telling someone the right time, for instance, making a correct diagnosis of a disease, expressing a genuine feeling, passing on sound advice, drawing apt analogies, giving illuminating examples, offering reliable opinions, making warranted interpretations. The ways in which any of those pieces of truth-telling is related to the states of affairs which support it and make it true are much more complex than the mere matching of a description with some observable facts.

Similarly, the connections between words and experience which are necessary if religious claims are to tell us anything true are not simple relations between a description and the facts it is taken to correspond to. The connection, if there is one, will be oblique and subtle, for it is not a direct matching between words and observable features of things, but an indirect one, mediated by signs, meaningful phenomena, events and experiences, all of which are interpreted in the attempt to distil from them information going beyond what they simply tell us in themselves. Religious doctrines, like the Christian ones, 'There exists only one God', 'Jesus is the Saviour of mankind', 'God has a plan for the world', 'The Holy Spirit proceeds from the Father and the Son', are not simple descriptions of the non-natural subject-matter they are about. They are complex abstractions, theoretical proposals, based on countless interpretations of empirical phenomena believed to mediate, through their meaningful occurrence and significance for human religious life, information about truths beyond them.

Much that has been said, in previous chapters, about the testing of religious *claims* must be seen in a new light when the interpretative basis of those claims is properly considered. It is far too simple an approach to treat questions about truth in religions as simply the question whether or not there is sufficient evidence to verify some supposedly descriptive doctrinal proposition or claim. What has to be tested is, rather, the apparent discovery of significance, the supposed grasping of meaningfulness in certain things which the language used in

104

those claims attempts to express and make some systematic sense of.[1]

The finding of observations more or less fitting the words used, the discovery of patterns in the data suggesting something like what the ideas and images of the language convey, should be seen as the *supporting of interpretations* rather than the verifying of assertions and the proving true of claims. A well-supported interpretation is still open to amendment; unlike a true proposition it does not claim to have the whole truth or say the final word. In the highly disputed field of supernatural realities, which religions take themselves to deal with, even the best-supported interpretation may still not count as a true description. The meaning it seems to grasp and express perhaps turns out to be well backed up by observations and experience. But at most that makes it a reliable guide or an appropriate model.

I have spoken throughout this book of religious *claims*, *assertions* or *statements*, since that is how they appear to those who make them as believers. But it may be more accurate, philosophically, to describe religious claims as *proposals* or *suggestions* (or even as theories or hypotheses, though the use of those terms may for some suggest too close an analogy with scientific testing procedures).[2]

I have accepted the view that if central religious claims or proposals are to carry information for mankind they must have some points of contact with human experience. If their truth (or falsity) makes no difference at all to what human beings can envisage, expect to meet with, or undergo in this or any other life, then they cannot be seriously regarded as the supremely important and profound claims to knowledge they have characteristically been taken to be. When attention is turned from the statements in religious language to the phenomena

[1] Some rather different senses of *true*, as in expressions like 'subjectively true' or 'existentially true', often appear in religious contexts. While such expressions have their uses, they generally confuse the issue when introduced into discussions of what truth (in a propositional or informative sense) there may be in religions, and for that reason I have not attempted to say anything about them.

[2] For a discussion of *suggestions* and *proposals* in religious discourse see William A. Christian, *Meaning and Truth in Religion*. Princeton University Press 1964.

which those statements purport to interpret, the basis for that approach becomes clearer. The question of religion's truth and informativeness can be seen as more extensive than merely looking for observational tests sufficient to verify some theological statement or doctrinal claim. The question has to be directed rather to the phenomena from which those claims arise, and the responses to those phenomena which the claims attempt to articulate.

Thus instead of asking 'Is belief in divine providence true?' (in the sense of 'Is there such a thing as divine providence?') we should ask rather: 'Do the kinds of event and experience religious believers look to when they talk about divine providence carry anything like the sort of significance for human belief and response which those people think they find in them, and express by talking about them in such language?' For that is what it would *mean* for belief in divine providence to be true. In other words, the first thing to be investigated, to evaluate the truth of religions, is not the truth or falsity of statements and claims made in religious language, but the interpretation of phenomena, mostly non-verbal, on which those claims rest. What is there about such things that has led people, on the strength of them, to speak in those ways? How, if at all, might those things support such interpretations and sustain such responses?

All that has been said above about the ways of testing religious claims has an important bearing on these questions. But the search for tests and relevant observations can now be seen as not so tightly tied to the verifying of certain fact-claiming utterances, and more loosely related to the evaluating of ways of regarding certain phenomena. It has generally been assumed that the validity of religious interpretations and responses depends on the truth of the doctrinal beliefs they reflect. But the order can just as well be reversed, so that the doctrines are taken to reflect the interpretations, rather than *vice versa*. What it means for the beliefs or the doctrines to be true, sound or well-founded, is that the interpretations they rest on are somehow or other supported by the phenomena to which they are directed, and indeed, in crucial cases, better supported than any of the alternative ways of responding to and making sense of those phenomena.

We have in past chapters looked briefly at the wide range

of phenomena which receive religious interpretations. We have mentioned this-worldly views of life which are enhanced by the non-cognitive use of religious stories (chapter three); events and experiences (from utterly extraordinary to quite mundane) in this life and perhaps also in some life to come, offered as circumstantial evidence that religious beliefs carry genuine informative content (chapters four and five); and appeals to some authoritative source of religious knowledge, backed up by arguments why we should take their word for things we cannot find out about ourselves (chapter six). We have noted how none of those possibilities can be properly assessed except in the context of the behaviour and ways of life of religious people (chapters seven and eight).

The main concern throughout has been to show how some degree of testability for religious claims is possible; to show that despite their oblique and elusive character religious beliefs and utterances can have informative content (thus meeting some of the objections to religious language discussed in chapters one and two). But deciding what informativeness religious claims have in fact, what truth they genuinely convey, is a far larger task, and one which philosophers of religion certainly ought not to consider tackling on their own. For a task like that the resources of all who investigate human religious interpretations, behaviour and phenomena must be called upon; and that includes those who know the interpretations thoroughly themselves, as sensitive participants in religious life, as well as those who are equally sensitive to alternative interpretations, both from other religious points of view, and from the points of view of those who do not live by any religion.

ON NOT HAVING THE LAST WORD

I have throughout taken as the chief worry of the philosopher the possibility of *illusory* meaningfulness in religious claims; the fear that the believer is misled, and misleads himself, by religious language which seems to carry great meaning, but which is in no way supported by fact. The central issue in our study of religious language, then, has been showing how there can be sufficient consistency with experience and openness to objective tests for at least the possibility of genuine informative content in religious claims. There is a further possibility, however, less often discussed in philosophy of religion, since little can be done about it apart from noting it as a possibility. There may be phenomena with meanings which would bear on religious questions and pursuits if they were recognized as such, yet which are thought irrelevant to religion simply because they are not appreciated; their significance slips through the net of existing religious conceptions. We have spoken of the danger of over-interpretation of things in religious words. What we are now considering is the possibility of their *under*-interpretation.

The extent of our understanding of things may depend very much on our knowledge of suitable words. Sometimes, for lack of the right words, a whole dimension of meaningfulness is missed; while finding new ways of combining words can help draw attention to unnoticed facts and their meanings. Consider how such recently coined phrases as 'male chauvinism', 'ecological imbalance' or 'black theology' have changed our appreciation of a whole range of things, actions and attitudes previously not found nearly so significant. Understanding and knowledge can grow, in religious matters no less than elsewhere, because of the endless possibilities of new forms of language-use. If there is truth within religions, and real significance for human life amongst the things religions deal with, that significance may not be anything like adequately reflected in the things religions have so far said, the doctrines they have up till now constructed.

The obscurity of religious language is in fact an advantage, so far as the possibilities of development go. For oblique language is always open to amendment and clarification, which can often take place without seriously negating or denying what was understood before. Religious traditions themselves have illustrated that time and again. Existing religious interpretations may, then, be reliable guides up to a point, without necessarily saying all there is to be said, or even saying what they do say in anything like the best, most accurate way.

It is a mistake to think there can be no meaning where people at a certain time and place in human history happen to find none. Many people doubtful about a future for religion point to the narrowness and naïvety of the religious interpretations of the majority of mankind up to the present day. But optimists about religion hold that our very recognition of the shortcomings of the past may give grounds for hope; they feel there is no good reason to assume that in the late twentieth century man cannot expect to come across anything further in the way of spiritual or religious significance for his life.[3] Whatever the future of religion may be, people will inevitably go on putting into words the things and experiences they believe to be deeply significant. And so long as they do, there will continue to be a point in attempts by the philosophically-minded to appreciate religious language and to understand more about its uses.

[3] With the possibility of yet-to-be-discovered religious significance in mind, some contemporary Christian theologians are exploring a number of matters of immediate human concern: racial equality, social justice, economic development, conservation of nature, women's liberation, revolution, work, leisure, mental health, and other subjects felt to have been neglected in traditional Christian theology. Of particular interest, too, for the next generation of religious believers throughout the world will be man's increasing understanding of other religious traditions, and no doubt a better appreciation will arise of similarities and differences in the interpretations world religions make of central human phenomena. The fact of plurality of interpretations may itself become a phenomenon open to religious interpretation in ways hardly conceived of in past religious traditions.

SHORT BIBLIOGRAPHY

Ayer, Alfred J., *Language, Truth and Logic*, 2nd edn Gollancz 1946.

Bevan, Edwyn, *Symbolism and Belief*. Fontana 1962.

Blackstone, W. T., *The Problem of Religious Knowledge*. Prentice-Hall 1963.

Christian, William A., *Meaning and Truth in Religion*. Princeton University Press 1964.

Dillistone, F. W., *Christianity and Symbolism*. Collins 1955.

Fawcett, Thomas, *The Symbolic Language of Religion*. S.C.M. Press 1970.

Flew, Antony, *God and Philosophy*. Hutchinson 1966.

Flew, Antony and MacIntyre, Alasdair, eds, *New Essays in Philosophical Theology*. S.C.M. Press 1955.

Hepburn, Ronald W., *Christianity and Paradox*. Watts 1958.

Hick, John, ed., *Faith and the Philosophers*. Macmillan 1966.

Hick, John, *Philosophy of Religion*. Prentice-Hall 1963.

Hook, Sydney, *Religious Experience and Truth*. Oliver and Boyd 1962.

Jeffner, Anders, *The Study of Religious Language*. S.C.M. Press 1972.

Lewis, H. D., *Philosophy of Religion*. English Universities Press 1965.

MacIntyre, Alasdair, ed., *Metaphysical Beliefs*. S.C.M. Press 1957.

Macquarrie, John, *God-Talk*. S.C.M. Press 1967.

Miles, T. R., *Religion and the Scientific Outlook*. Allen and Unwin 1959.

Mitchell, Basil, *The Justification of Religious Belief*. Macmillan 1973.

Mitchell, Basil, ed., *The Philosophy of Religion*. Oxford University Press 1971.

Nielsen, Kai, *Contemporary Critiques of Religion*. Macmillan 1971.

Penelhum, Terence, *Problems of Religious Knowledge*. Macmillan 1971.

Phillips, D. Z., *The Concept of Prayer*. Routledge and Kegan Paul 1965.

Phillips, D. Z., ed., *Faith and Philosophical Enquiry*. Routledge and Kegan Paul 1970.

Price, H. H., *Belief*. Allen and Unwin 1969.

Ramsey, Ian T., *Religious Language*. S.C.M. Press 1957.

Smart, Ninian, *Philosophy of Religion*. Random House 1970.

Trigg, Roger, *Reason and Commitment*. Cambridge University Press 1973.

Vesey, G. N. A., ed., *Talk of God* (Royal Institute of Philosophy Lectures 1967-8), Macmillan 1969.

Wittgenstein, Ludwig, *Philosophical Investigations*, tr. G. E. M. Anscombe. Blackwell 1958.

INDEX

P 430

DATE DUE

F			
JY 16'84			
NOV 19 '86			
GAYLORD			PRINTED IN U.S.A.